792
.09
TAY

170μ6

GREEK ANI

Acting and the

GREEK AND ROMAN TOPICS

Series Editor: Robin Barrow

Sparta
Robin Barrow

Athletics, Sports and Games
John Murrell

Acting and the Stage
David Taylor

BY THE SAME AUTHOR:
Cicero and Rome, Macmillan, 1973

Acting and the Stage

DAVID TAYLOR
Formerly Head of Classics Department,
Watford Boys' Grammar School

UNWIN HYMAN

Published by
UNWIN HYMAN LIMITED
15–17 Broadwick Street
London W1V 1FP

First published in 1978 by
George Allen & Unwin (Publishers) Ltd
Reprinted 1985, 1986
Reprinted by Unwin Hyman Publishers Limited 1988, 1989

© George Allen & Unwin (Publishers) Ltd 1978

All rights reserved. No part of this publication may be reproduced, stored in a
retrieval system, or transmitted in any form or by any means, electronic,
mechanical, photocopying, recording, or otherwise, without the prior permission of
Unwin Hyman Limited.

British Library Cataloguing in Publication Data

Taylor, David, b.1945
  Acting and the stage. – (Greek and Roman
topics).
  1. Theater – Greece 2. Theater – Rome
I. Title II. Series
792′.0938   PA 3201   77–30595

ISBN 0–04–930008–3

For Penelope

Printed in Great Britain
by Bell & Bain Ltd Glasgow

Contents

Illustrations

Preface

Limitations of space impose compression, and on occasion conclusions are more tentative than the text may suggest. However, where a major point relies on guesswork or invention, this is stated.

I should like to record grateful thanks to Mrs Pat Easterling of Newnham College, Cambridge, for many helpful suggestions (though she cannot be held responsible for any of the views expressed), and to my wife, whose practical experience of the theatre and assistance with the preparation of the manuscript at all stages have been invaluable.

Acknowledgements

The author and publishers are grateful to the following for permission to reproduce illustrations:
British Museum: cover, 1, 16, 20, 27, 28. The Mansell Collection: 3, 4, 5, 6, 7, 11, 12, 13, 15, 18, 19, 22, 23, 24, 25, 26, 29, 30, 32. Ian Murray: 21. The National Tourist Organisation of Greece: 31. David Raeburn, Headmaster, Whitgift School: 17. University of London, Warburg Institute: 9, 10.

1 How the Greek Theatre Began

What is an actor? An actor is someone who adopts a character which is not his own, to suit the part he is playing. Sometimes he wears a special costume. In the circus, clowns wear padded clothing and heavy make-up. In some theatrical productions actors wear masks and elaborate costumes, which are a reminder of the earliest days of the theatre. Actors in ancient Greece, where the theatre really began, always hid their real personalities under a mask and costume. Because of this, the Greek audiences did not expect actors to be like ordinary people. They expected something different.

DIFFERENT EXPECTATIONS

'Different expectations' is a useful idea to keep in mind when reading this book. The theatre is certainly not exactly the same as it was in ancient Greece – but it has not changed completely. If we could not understand the words of the plays which the Greeks and Romans watched, we would find them very confusing. But even if you do not understand Latin or Greek, there are English translations available. Of course, people do change over the ages. Not all societies find the same things funny, sad or cruel. Today's audiences may not react to Greek and Roman plays as audiences once did. But there are many links between the ancient and modern theatre. Audiences still admire heroes and hate villains, even if the heroes and villains themselves have changed.

THE MAGIC OF THE THEATRE

The theatre and acting have always had a special appeal for many people. When acting was not considered a respectable occupation for girls, some defied their parents in order to go on the stage. Actors themselves have often been given 'star' treatment – long before the days of Hollywood and film stars.

Today acting also plays a much more important part in schools. Once children sat through their lessons in absolute silence, except when chanting tables. Now, teachers use classroom drama to encourage children to express themselves, work with others, and think about situations and characters.

Not everyone likes to stand up and perform in front of other people; some of us find it frightening or embarrassing. But the theatre also caters for those who prefer to be 'behind the scenes'. Building sets, making costumes, prompting, stage-managing — there are many jobs which make theatrical productions a success, but which do not put people into the limelight. This book will provide information about the Greek and Roman theatre, but it should also give you some ideas about how to set about producing plays, complete with actors, scenery, costumes, music and props. After all, the word 'drama' (a Greek word) means 'doing', not 'watching' or 'reading'.

THE BEGINNINGS OF THE THEATRE

Many books have been written about how the theatre began. They do not always tell the same story. There is no really straight-forward explanation. Nobody knows exactly where the idea of performing in front of other people first came from. The easy way out is to say that the important thing is the plays themselves, and therefore it does not matter how the theatre began. Still, it is worth trying to discover what we can.

EXAMINING THE EVIDENCE

How might we find out the answer? We could look at the plays themselves, but this does not take us very far. The Greek play-wrights were writing plays, not a history of the theatre. What about other Greek writers, such as historians? (After all, the Greeks invented history, as well as the theatre.) This is sometimes useful, but not as often as we might hope. Greek historians dealt mainly with wars and politics.

Much useful information comes, in fact, from Greek art. There are many examples of painted vases and sculpture which date from the time when the theatre began. So this book has a number of illustrations which are taken from Greek vases and sculptures.

GREEK ART

Exhibit A is a vase from the area around Athens, the city where all the great playwrights lived. Several vases were made around 500 BC (that is, in the very early days of the theatre) which show groups of men dressed up in bird or animal costumes to take part in revels — dancing and general merrymaking. This one shows a man playing a small wind instrument (like a double oboe), accompanying two dancers dressed in a costume with wings, feathers and a bird's head. Choruses of costumed dancers

. B

1 Bird-Men

therefore go back to the beginnings of the theatre, and clearly they contributed to its development. Nearly a hundred years later than this vase-painting, a play called *The Birds* had a chorus wearing costumes very similar to these. This play survives today.

INSCRIPTIONS

We can also look at Greek inscriptions. These are records inscribed on stone. Some of them contain information about the plays and playwrights, and the years when plays were first produced. Sometimes complete inscriptions still exist; there are also many fragments, such as *Exhibit B*.

Exhibit B is part of a list, called *The Athenian Victors' List*, which records the names of winners in the dramatic competitions at Athens. There are no complete names on this portion, but scholars have been able to work out some interesting facts. The Greek capital letters are

2 The Athenian Victors' List

very clear. The top line has the letters ΣXY, the middle letters of the name Ae*schy*lus. (The Greek alphabet is given in Appendix C.) The fifth line reads ΚΛΗΣ ΔΙΙΙΙ. This is the end of the name Sopho*cles*, and after the name are Greek numerals – ten, five and three ones, totalling eighteen.

Aeschylus and Sophocles are two of the most famous Greek playwrights, and these records must refer to them. The Victors' List went back about ten years before the name Aeschylus, but the first few entries cannot be read now. A later Greek writer says that Aeschylus won his first victory in the playwrights' competition in about 484 BC, and this fits other information in the records. Sophocles won his first victory later than Aeschylus, and altogether won eighteen victories.

Exhibit A and Exhibit B are just two examples of evidence from Greek art and inscriptions. There are many others, and we can add these to the writings of the Greeks, and the surviving remains of the theatre buildings. In this way, it is possible to build up quite a full picture of the early days of the theatre, but there are still some things about which we cannot be sure, because the evidence is not conclusive.

GREEK FESTIVALS

A festival is a regular celebration of an important event, normally a religious event. Our best-known annual festival is Christmas, celebrating the birth of Christ. Countries such as Greece and Italy still have many annual festivals, just as the Greeks and Romans did in ancient times. Festivals are times when no work is done, and they often include great processions through the streets, with dancing, drinking and general merriment. Sometimes a statue of the saint or god to whom the festival is dedicated is carried through the streets. The festivals of ancient Greece were rather like this, and as the Greeks had many different gods, each one had his festivals.

DIONYSUS

The god Dionysus had four annual festivals in Athens. They were the *Anthesteria*, the *Lenaia*, the *Country Dionysia* and the *Great Dionysia*.

Dionysus was a strange god. He was the son of Zeus, but not by his wife, the goddess Hera. Zeus had many affairs with mortal women, and one of these was Semele, the mother of Dionysus. In anger, Hera had Semele killed by the thunderbolt of Zeus. But Zeus rescued Semele's unborn child, and hid him from Hera in his thigh – from where he was eventually born. Despite this odd beginning, Dionysus became one of the most frequently worshipped of all the Greek gods.

Dionysus is often shown in paintings as the god of wine, like the Roman god Bacchus. He is either drinking wine, or sur-

3 Dionysus at sea. The artist has imagined a vine trailing round the mast of Dionysus' ship, with bunches of grapes suspended above the sail

rounded by grapes, as on the painting which shows him sailing in his ship (illustration 3). But he was more than this. He was especially connected with fertility, whether human birth or the fruitfulness of the land. Many early religious festivals, like our Harvest Festival, are associated with sowing seed or gathering in the crops. Such festivals were particularly important to the ancient Greeks, who lived almost completely on agricultural produce, in a land which is not very fertile. Everything depended on a good harvest in the small cultivated plains which lay between the barren mountains.

One such festival was the Great Dionysia. This was held every March, when the seas were open to sailing again after the winter storms, and when farmers were hoping for success with their summer crops. It was a great occasion in Athens, and people came from all over Greece to take part in it. This festival was the main occasion when plays were presented, and it is described in the next chapter. Since both the Country Dionysia and the Lenaia also included plays, it is clear that the theatre was connected with the worship of Dionysus.

Dionysus had many devoted followers, in particular a band of women known as *Bacchantes* or *Maenads*. At certain times of year, these women abandoned their homes, ran to the mountains and took part in frenzied worship of their god. The climax was a meal of raw flesh. They believed that by eating this they lost their own personalities, and took on the power and person of the god. The worshippers often wore masks, and the image of the god was in the form of a mask on a pole, draped in a long robe (see illustration 18). Here is another link between Dionysus and the Greek theatre. The actors also become another person, and they wear a mask.

THE GREEK PLAYS

The link with Dionysus is also seen in the different types of Greek play.

Satyr-plays

These were a peculiarly Greek kind of play, probably the earliest plays of all. *Satyrs* were strange wood-creatures in Greek legends. They behaved like beasts, and are always drawn with animal features. They became associated with other legendary creatures called *Silenoi*, and satyr-plays always had a chorus of satyrs or Silenoi. One satyr-play which survives today is *Cyclops*, by Euripides. It tells the famous story of how Odysseus blinded the one-eyed giant Polyphemus, which Euripides adapted from Homer's epic tale, the *Odyssey*. In the play, the chorus of Silenoi,

4 Silenos

under their leader Silenos, play a large part, although they are not mentioned in Homer's version of the story. Silenos is often represented in Greek art – look at the splendid sculpture on this page. In the legends, he and the rest of the Silenoi became the followers of Dionysus, and they are often to be seen making or drinking his wine.

Tragedies

Even if you do not know much about the Greek theatre, you have probably met the word 'tragedy'. To us, 'tragedy' means misfortune or disaster. If a play is called a tragedy, we expect it to have an unhappy end. But originally the word 'tragedy' meant something quite different. The Greek word is τραγῳδία and means 'goat-song'. This seems a strange thing to call a play. It used to be thought that the original goat-singers were a chorus in goatskin costume, rather like satyrs. But it is more likely that the chorus received this name because they competed at the festival of Dionysus for the prize of a goat. In either case, the origins of tragedy belong with the worship of Dionysus.

Comedies
The word 'comedy' is also familiar to us. We think of comedy as something which makes people laugh. Comedy also comes from a Greek word, κωμῳδία, which means 'the song of the merrymakers (revellers)'. These revellers behaved and sang in a happy, festive manner, so the word has not changed its meaning very much. Fancy-dress was a common feature of revels, as we saw from Exhibit A (page 10). Revellers accompanied processions at the beginning of the festivals of Dionysus. They welcomed the god's arrival in the city, singing and dancing in high spirits.

THE FIRST ACTORS

All three types of play, then, developed from the worship of Dionysus, with choruses who performed in honour of the god. But what about actors? So far, nothing has been said about them. This is not a mistake. The theatre actually did start without any separate actors; there was only the chorus. But now it is time to look at how acting began, and how the plays developed from these beginnings.

THESPIS

Even today actors are sometimes called Thespians. The name comes from Thespis, a Greek who can be regarded as the true founder of the theatre. Thespis won the prize (a goat) when tragedy was first performed at the Great Dionysia, in about 534 BC. From this time, performances of tragedy were an annual part of the festival, and it soon also contained satyr-plays and comedies. Thespis introduced an individual actor who had conversations with the chorus-leader, and spoke a prologue to the audience, explaining what was going to happen. Without this step, there would have been no theatre as we know it. (The Greek word for actor was ὑποκριτής, meaning 'answerer'. It has given us the word 'hypocrite' – someone who pretends to be something he is not, an insincere person.)

AESCHYLUS

The next change came with the playwright Aeschylus, whose picture is on page 16. He introduced a second actor. Before this, the one actor could only speak to the chorus-leader, a very important

5 Aeschylus (526–456 BC)

person in the performance. Now the two actors could speak to each other, and present scenes without involving the chorus. This gave playwrights much more scope for creating characters.

SOPHOCLES

The second playwright shown here (illustration 6) is Sophocles, who went one step further than Aeschylus by introducing a third actor. In the Greek theatre of the fifth century BC there were never more than three actors in one play. But more than three characters could appear in a play, provided they were not all on stage at the same time. All the actor had to do was change his costume and mask, and he became a new character. The chorus-leader continued to join in the dialogue, and there were often silent 'extras' as well.

6 Sophocles (496–406 BC)   7 Euripides (485–406 BC)

Nobody really knows why there was this limit of three actors. However, in the early days of the theatre there were no professional actors, who made their living from the theatre as actors do today. Actors had to be trained specially for the festival, and therefore it was cheaper and easier only to have to deal with a small number.

EURIPIDES

The third statue (illustration 7) portrays Euripides, the last of the great writers of Greek tragedy whose works have come down to the present day. Euripides was about ten years younger than Sophocles, but they often competed against each other in the Festival of the Great Dionysia. Although Euripides made changes in the style of tragedy, he did not introduce any more actors.

Each of these three writers composed many plays that have not survived to the present day, but those that have survived are given in Appendix B. We have nineteen plays by Euripides, compared with only seven by Aeschylus and Sophocles.

SUMMARY

Here is a summary of the main conclusions we have reached about how the theatre began:

1 The Greeks introduced three kinds of play for the theatre: *satyr-play*, *tragedy* and *comedy*.
2 These were all connected with the worship of Dionysus, a god of fertility who was worshipped by many followers (particularly women), and who had four festivals at Athens.
3 Greek plays started from choruses who sang at the festivals of Dionysus. Some of the choruses wore strange costumes repsenting satyrs, animals or birds.
4 Towards the end of the sixth century BC, a competition for tragedy was introduced at the *Great Dionysia*. The first contest was won by Thespis. Later, the competitions included satyr-plays and comedies as well.
5 *Thespis* introduced the first actor, *Aeschylus* the second, and *Sophocles* the third. Three became the regular number in all types of play.

2 The Festival of the Great Dionysia

The main festival at which plays were performed was the Great Dionysia, held in Athens in March every year. How was this festival organised? What form did the competition take? What did the Greek theatre look like? Who came to see the plays? Who paid for the performances? This chapter will be answering these and other questions, using as an example the year 441 BC. In this year, according to most experts, one of Sophocles' most famous plays, *Antigone*, was first performed, and we shall be looking at the preparations for this. The actual performance is described in the next chapter.

THE THEATRE OF DIONYSUS

The oldest theatre in Greece is the theatre of Dionysus at Athens, and it was here that *Antigone* received its first performance. The theatre was part of the area dedicated to the god Dionysus, with temples and shrines in his honour. It was on the slopes of the *Acropolis*, the hill in the centre of Athens. On the Acropolis still stands the famous temple in honour of Athene, the *Parthenon*, built in the fifth century BC. The Acropolis rises steeply from the plains below, and the Athenians had originally used it as a defence against invaders. But now it was the religious centre of the city, and a natural site for the first theatre.

The Greeks always built their theatres in the open air. The builders used the natural curve of hillsides for the seating area. One reason for this was that they discovered that such sites often provided superb acoustics, which designers ever since have envied. Right from the back of the huge theatres, every sound is clearly audible.

The theatre of Dionysus, like other Greek theatres, can still be visited, but it has changed since the days of Sophocles. A recent photograph (illustration 12, page 27) shows how it looks now. But to see what it looked like when *Antigone* was first performed, we need to take away the later additions, as on the plan shown here.

The spectators' seats are in a curving area, a little more than a semi-circle, and slope down to the centre. The Greeks called this the ϑέατρον (*theatron*), from which our word 'theatre' comes. At the time of the first production of *Antigone*, the seats were probably wooden, but soon afterwards they were replaced by stone seats. Between 10,000 and 20,000 people crowded in for the performances. The complete circle (shown on the plan), in the middle of the

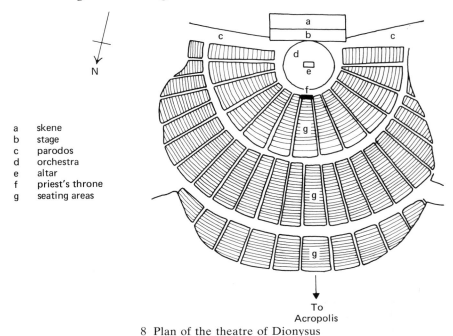

a   skene
b   stage
c   parodos
d   orchestra
e   altar
f   priest's throne
g   seating areas

8 Plan of the theatre of Dionysus

seating area is the *orchestra*. This Greek word has also come into our language with a change of meaning. For the Greeks it was the *dancing-place*, where the chorus performed their songs and dances, and were often joined by the actors. In the *orchestra* there was an altar to Dionysus, a reminder of the theatre's religious function. Sometimes the plots of the plays contained religious ceremonies which were performed at this altar.

Behind was the *skene* (stage-building), from which the English word 'scene' comes. This was a wooden building where actors could change, and it also served as the background for the play, as a house, a temple or a palace. The front wall of the *skene* had a large double door which opened for actors to make their entrances, and there were probably two smaller doors as well, one on each side. The action of the play always took place out of doors, unlike most modern plays.

In front of the stage-building was a low wooden platform or stage, on which actors could stand, with steps leading down to the *orchestra*. From this the actors could easily speak with the chorus. Actors entered the theatre either from the stage-building or from a *parodos* (side-entrance) if they were arriving from another place. There were two side-entrances, one on each side of the *orchestra*, and the chorus made their entry from one of these.

The theatre had three possible levels for actors: the platform in front of the stage-building, the *orchestra*, and the roof of the stage-building, which was reached by steps from inside.

THE CHOREGOS

Apart from the playwright, the most important person concerned with the preparations for the festival was the *choregos* (sponsor). We are going to look at the tasks of the sponsor who worked with Sophocles in 441 BC. His name is not known, but a few years earlier there was a sponsor called Bion, so we shall use this name.

APPOINTING THE SPONSORS

Each new year in Athens, a fresh set of officials took up their positions. Among these were ten men appointed to the position of *archon* (senior magistrate), and one of these was to select three sponsors from among the wealthiest Athenian citizens. The sponsors had to help the city by undertaking certain public duties, as a kind of tax on their wealth. When Bion was appointed, he could have asked to be excused if he was performing another of these duties, such as paying for the equipment of a warship. But in fact he welcomed the appointment, since it gave him an opportunity to display his wealth in a good cause. There were three sponsors for the tragic competition, one for each playwright selected to take part. Lots were drawn to decide which sponsor worked with which playwright.

THE DUTIES OF THE SPONSORS

Bion's main duties, as a sponsor, were concerned with the chorus. In tragedies, this was a group of fifteen men who had to be trained to learn their words, music and dances, which formed an important part of the plays. The judges paid a great deal of attention to their performance, and noted how well or badly they had been trained.

Each tragic playwright had one day to present four plays. These were performed one after another – three tragedies followed by a satyr-play. This meant that the chorus had to learn four sets of words, and wear four different costumes, for which Bion was to find the money.

Bion was therefore the financial backer. He had to pay the wages of the chorus, and hire the musician who accompanied them on the double-oboe. Any special effects of scenery had to be paid for as well. There were not many of these, but as Sophocles invented *skene*-painting, he may have wanted a specially painted background for *Antigone* and his other plays.

Bion did not train the chorus himself, but Sophocles, as it happened, was an expert on the art of the chorus (he even wrote a book about it). He had also acted in some of his own plays, but had retired from acting because of trouble with his voice. Without Sophocles to train the chorus, Bion would have had to hire an expert trainer.

THE ACTORS

The sponsor had no say in the selection and training of the three actors, but he took a keen interest in their progress: in several scenes the chorus and actors worked closely together. A few years earlier, in 449 BC, the Athenians introduced a prize for the best actor, for which only the three *protagonists* (leading actors) were eligible; this was added to the prize for the best playwright, and made competition much keener. Good actors could help a poor play, while bad ones could ruin an excellent play.

The magistrate drew lots to decide which of the three chosen leading actors acted for which tragic playwright. So although the leading actor had a principal role in each of his four plays, Sophocles had absolutely no control over this important decision. However, he could choose his own *deuteragonist* (second actor) and *tritagonist* (third actor). We know that a man called *Heracleides* was once leading actor for Sophocles. And Sophocles himself often chose *Tlepolemos* to act for him, while another actor called *Dicaiarchos* also used to appear in his plays. This book therefore will give these names to the actors who performed for Sophocles in 441 BC, although they are only guesses. As these names, like some others in this book, are rather awkward to pronounce, a guide is given in Appendix A (page 72).

COSTUMES

Costumes were extremely important in enabling the actors to show the audience what character they were playing. It is not clear exactly what costumes were like in Sophocles' time, since (like the theatres) they changed later. But we can look at helpful illustrations from vases painted not long after *Antigone* was written. One of these (on page 43) is a painting of women worshipping Dionysus. The god is in the centre, represented by a pillar covered by a mask and a decorated robe, with a long pleated skirt underneath. Another vase-painting (illustration 9) shows an actor wearing a highly decorated costume and holding a mask. He is actually preparing for a satyr-play, but the tragic costume must have been very much like this. Putting the two together, it seems that the tragic costume developed from the robe of Dionysus.

It consisted of a full-length robe covered by a shorter cloak, which came below the knees. The sleeves were long and full, and there were various decorations such as stripes, spirals or animal shapes. However, actors playing the part of poor men or women wore plain costumes, and characters in mourning wore black robes. The tragic mask, which was always worn, together with the soft leather calf-length boots, made up the complete costume.

This style of dress made it far easier for men to take women's parts,

9 The actor's costume

which they had to do as there were no actresses in the Greek theatre.
(The same was true in Shakespeare's time.) Hairy arms and legs were
hidden, and a female mask completed the disguise.

MASKS

At the time of the first performance of *Antigone*, tragic masks looked
quite natural, like those in illustrations 9 and 10. To make it easier for
all the audience to see actors' faces, the eyes and the mouth were

10 An actor with his mask

slightly exaggerated, and the mask, which fitted over the whole head, was rather larger than life. Masks were usually made of linen, but sometimes cork or wood was used. They had lifelike hair, long or short, and of various colours. An opening in the mouth made it possible for the actors to be heard clearly, with the help of the excellent natural acoustics. There were also eye-holes to enable them to see. Greeks did not expect actors to imitate people in real life as we do, but the masks and costumes still had to allow them to move and speak easily and clearly. They also made it possible for the audience to distinguish one character from another from the back of the theatre. There were no opera-glasses in those days.

But masks do present the actor with one difficulty. He cannot express feelings by using his face. In films or television plays, close-up shots can show what a character is supposed to be feeling without any words or movement. But a masked actor cannot use his face to express laughter or crying, astonishment or horror. Apart from his own gestures and movements, he must rely on tone of voice and the words of the play. But Greek audiences were used to using their imagination, and perhaps this lack of facial expression did not worry them.

ADVERTISING THE PLAYS

You might think that it would have been difficult for playwrights to let people know about their plays in advance, without modern methods of advertising. But Athens was a small city by our standards. In addition, the preparations took place out of doors, as there were no suitable indoor halls. Rehearsals were probably public occasions, with opportunities for passers-by to watch the actors and chorus at work. Rival sponsors may have had their spies out. What was Sophocles planning this year? In Athens, news spread fast. Perhaps publicity for playwrights was actually easier than it is today. With all our methods of communication, how many new plays have you heard of this year? Where would you find the information?

There was also a special occasion in Athens just before the festival began, when Sophocles and Bion, and their rivals, gave people an idea of what to expect. Each playwright brought along his actors, who were not wearing their costumes and masks, but had garlands to suit the festival atmosphere, and they told the assembled crowds the subjects of the plays.

THE AUDIENCE

The people took a great interest in the preparations for the festival, and the theatre was packed for performances. What sort of people watched the plays?

The majority were Athenian citizens – rich as well as poor, the well educated as well as those who could scarcely read or write. (To be a citizen of Athens you had to be a man, and also the son of a citizen.) There were also people living in Athens who came from other parts of Greece, and many visitors came especially for the festival, making their first sea voyage of the new season. Young men and boys attended, and so did some women, according to references in the plays, though probably not many: most Athenians thought a woman's place was at home. Slaves were probably not allowed to attend. Many plays introduced slaves as characters, but they were acted by citizens.

There was fierce competition for seats. Entry was by ticket, which controlled the numbers admitted. Many tickets made of bronze, ivory, lead or bone have been discovered. They did not have a seat number, but showed which block of seating the ticket-holder was to sit in. Individual seats could not be numbered in a theatre of this kind, but the seating area was divided into a number of wedge-shaped blocks. The ten tribes of Athenian citizens all had their own blocks, and there were special seats at the front of the theatre for important people. One belonged to the priest of Dionysus, who sat in the front row. In one comedy, an actor playing the god Dionysus came right across the *orchestra* and appealed to the priest to rescue him from danger. He promised to buy the priest a drink after the show if he helped him. The priest's throne is shown in illustration 11. The Greek inscription can be made out clearly. The first word, IEPEΩΣ, means 'priest', and the second, ΔIONYΣOY, means 'of Dionysus'.

We do not know how people obtained tickets, but the price was two *obols*. This was a small sum, but in any case, those poor people who

11 The throne of the priest of Dionysus

applied to their local authorities for a ticket were admitted free. The authorities then paid the fee to the official in charge of the theatre buildings.

As the festival approached, the excitement rose. The atmosphere must have been rather like that on a big sporting occasion today, as the visitors streamed in from all over the place to the large open-air arena. This was an event which happened only once a year, and for some visitors, only once in a lifetime.

THE START OF THE FESTIVAL

So the opening of the festival arrived. Bion and Sophocles had done all they could. Final rehearsals had been held. Everyone, it was hoped, knew the words and the dances. No expense had been spared with the costumes and masks for the chorus and actors. Bion had encouraged his friends to attend and cheer for Sophocles. This was his only chance of success with *Antigone* and the other plays. After the first performance, there was no long run, as there is in West End productions in London today. The following year, win or lose, Sophocles would be back (if he was picked) with four new plays.

12 The theatre of Dionysus as it is today

THE FIRST DAY

The festival began with a great procession. Sacrifices were offered to Dionysus, including the bull which was led in the procession. The scene was very colourful. Bion and the other sponsors dressed in magnificent gowns, and many other visitors wore brightly coloured clothes. Even those who had not got tickets took part in the festival as the procession made its noisy, merry way through the streets.

After the sacrifices came the first competitions. There were no actors in these, but large numbers of men and boys took part in choral recitations and dancing. Then came the evening, time for the *komos*, or revel, when lively singing and dancing in honour of Dionysus carried on late into the night.

THE ACTING COMPETITIONS

The next three days were devoted to the plays. At the time of Sophocles the pattern was probably as follows:

The second day. The first tragic playwright produced his four plays – three tragedies and a satyr-play. These began early in the morning and went on, with short breaks, for perhaps six hours. Then there was an interval, when people ate their lunches, which they usually brought with them (though snacks were also on sale in the theatre). Afterwards there was a single comedy, by the first of the comic playwrights. The order of playwrights was decided by lot. (We are going to imagine that Sophocles was drawn to go first in 441 BC.) The first plays may have made a stronger impact on the excited audience, but those on the last day would be freshest in the minds of the judges.

The third day. The second tragic and comic writers produced their plays, in the same order.

The fourth day. The third and final group of five plays was presented.

The fifth day. The judging of the best playwright and actor in each section, comedy and tragedy, took place, and prizes were presented.

It may seem amazing that audiences sat, on uncomfortable seats, through a total of fifteen plays in three days. But many people today switch on a television set at five o'clock in the evening and watch it until midnight. They watch from the comfort of their own armchairs, of course, but the Greeks were far more used to hard outdoor conditions. Furthermore, the plays were part of a great religious festival, and the audiences knew there would be no more until the next one. So they were prepared to make an effort – like people today who flock to such occasions as the Bayreuth Festival when Wagner's *Ring* cycle of operas is performed, or to pop festivals when a famous group makes a rare appearance.

In the next chapter we shall be looking in detail at the performance of *Antigone*, on the second day of the festival. But now we will look at the arrangements for judging the competitions.

THE DAY OF JUDGEMENT

After their own performance, Sophocles, Bion, the actors and the chorus had two full days to watch the entries of the other two tragic playwrights, and enjoy the light relief offered by the comedies in the afternoon. But then the festival moved towards its climax.

Beforehand, a list of a hundred names was drawn up, ten from each tribe of citizens. Each tribe was given an urn into which tablets bearing the ten names were placed. These were not to be interfered with. The names were those of ordinary Athenians; they did not have to be experts.

Just before the first play began, the magistrate drew out one name from each urn, and the ten men who were selected in this way (one from each tribe) swore solemnly that they would judge fairly. On the fifth day, after all the plays had been presented, each judge wrote on another tablet his order of merit for the three playwrights, and the ten tablets were placed in an urn again. Five were drawn out, and the writer who had most votes was declared the winner. We do not know much about the judging of the actors' competition, but the method was probably similar.

Everything was carefully designed to avoid cheating, but even so there were attempts to influence the judging. A sponsor might try to bribe the judges, or get his friends on to the original list. Sometimes trials were held after the festival to investigate incidents of this kind. The judges themselves did not have to say why they voted as they did, simply which playwright they liked best. Even with all these precautions the system was not perfect, but the fact that Sophocles won eighteen times may give some indication that often the judges picked the best playwright. It was a very democratic system, as we might expect in Athens, the city which founded democracy. It meant that ordinary people were closely involved in the festival. In fact, with all the actors, members of choruses, judges and magistrates, as well as the audiences, a very high proportion of the 40,000 or so Athenian citizens must have taken part.

THE END OF THE FESTIVAL

After the judging came the prize-giving ceremonies, when the winning playwright and actor were presented with a wreath, and a prize of money – we do not know how much. In 441 BC, Sophocles won the playwrights' competition, and there is a story that because of the popularity *Antigone* brought him, he was appointed to the important post of general the next year. He was quite a wealthy man, like many of the playwrights, and the money mattered less than the prestige. For the successful leading actor there was an automatic opportunity to act in the following year's festival, while the sponsor who had financed the winning plays could set up a monument to record his victory. Some of these still stand today.

When the festival had finished, the Athenian citizens held an Assembly, and carefully examined the way the magistrate had organised everything. If they disapproved, he could be fined. And then it was all over. Citizens went back to their normal occupations, and the playwrights started thinking about plays for the next festival. Perhaps the losing playwrights did not even keep their scripts. But some plays lived on, especially those by Aeschylus, Sophocles and Euripides, ready to be revived in the next century.

13 Masks for the Greek theatre. Mask (a) is for a young girl (like Antigone), and mask (b) shows a king (like Agamemnon or Oedipus). The others are for satyr-plays or comedies – compare mask (c) with the picture of Silenos on page 14

3   First Performance of Antigone

CHOICE OF SUBJECT

Unlike modern writers, Sophocles did not have a completely free hand in his choice of subject matter. Practically all tragedies dealt with Greek myths and legends. (There is only one real exception among surviving plays. *The Persians*, by Aeschylus, describes the victory of the Greeks over King Xerxes of Persia.)

One or two explanations can be given of why the writers kept using the same themes. First, the Greeks took stories of their early heroes far more seriously than we take legends such as 'King Arthur and the Round Table' and 'Robin Hood' – although even these are often used in plays and films. The Greeks learnt Homer's poems, the *Iliad* and the *Odyssey*, from a very early age. Many Athenians could quote long sections from them. The heroes of the poems, the legendary figures of the Trojan War (Achilles, Agamemnon, Odysseus and others), often feature in the tragedies. Other plays have heroes from the royal houses of such Greek cities as Mycenae and Thebes. (According to the legends, both houses suffered terrible disasters.)

Secondly, the festivals were, as we have seen, religious occasions. The Greeks believed that the gods had once mingled freely with mortals, and they often feature in the plays. These legendary stories were therefore not simply fairy tales. Questions about religion and morality often occurred in the legends, and the playwrights explored these questions. How should men act towards the gods and towards their fellow-men? Should one murder always be avenged by another? Issues of this kind constantly concerned the tragic playwrights.

The Greeks did not think that playwrights were unoriginal if they dealt with a familiar story. Instead, they admired the ways in which the playwrights could use the same stories to express different ideas. All three of the great tragic writers – Aeschylus, Sophocles and Euripides – wrote plays about Electra and Orestes, the daughter and son of Agamemnon and Clytemnestra (the king and queen of Mycenae). These three plays told the story of how Electra and Orestes planned to murder their mother because she had killed Agamemnon on his return from Troy. But the plays are very different from one another.

The choice of Antigone, daughter of Oedipus (the legendary king of Thebes), was in line with Sophocles' usual subjects – two of his other surviving plays also deal with Oedipus and Thebes. It was not, therefore, the story itself which made Sophocles' play original, but the way he treated the story.

THE PLAY'S BACKGROUND

When King Oedipus learnt that he had killed his father and married his mother (without realising what he had done), he blinded himself and gave up the throne of Thebes. He went into exile. His brother-in-law, Creon, ruled the city until Oedipus' two sons were old enough to reign. When they grew up, the sons quarrelled over which should be king, and the younger led an army against the city of Thebes. To settle the dispute, seven men were chosen from each side, including the two brothers. They had to fight each other in single combat. But in the critical battle, the brothers killed each other, leaving Creon as king. The invading army retreated from Thebes.

The legend was familiar to some of the audience, but many knew only the title of the play. There were no programme notes to tell them who the characters or actors were. Everything had to be worked out from the play. However, unlike the audience, we are in a position to look at a list of the characters in *Antigone*.

THE CHARACTERS

Characters

Antigone } Ismene }	daughters of Oedipus
Creon	king of Thebes
Eurydice	his wife, the queen
Haimon	son of Creon and Eurydice
Teiresias	a blind prophet
Guard	
Messenger	
Chorus	respected Theban citizens
Extras:	soldiers, servants, boy leading Teiresias

The first striking thing about this list is that there are eight speaking characters to be played by three actors; also, three characters are female. We have seen that costumes and masks made things easier, but even so the actors must have had a busy and difficult time. It is not surprising that Sophocles wanted the best possible actors, since they had to be able to change their voices and acting style convincingly to create new characters.

Obviously the same actor could not play two characters who were

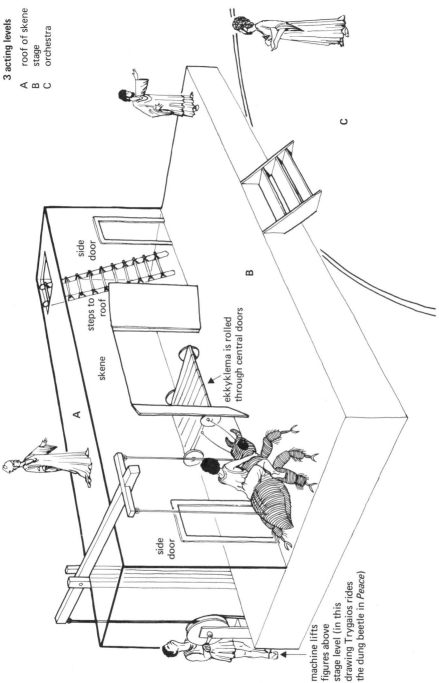

3 acting levels

A   roof of skene
B   stage
C   orchestra

side door

steps to roof

skene

ekkyklema is rolled through central doors

side door

machine lifts figures above stage level (in this drawing Trygaios rides the dung beetle in *Peace*)

14   The stage and stage-building (*skene*), showing the *mechane* and *ekkyklema*, and the three acting levels

on stage at the same time, but this still leaves several possible combinations. Though we cannot be certain, the following arrangement works well:

Heracleides (*protagonist*): Creon
Tlepolemos (*deuteragonist*): Antigone, Haimon, Messenger
Dicaiarchos (*tritagonist*): Ismene, Guard, Teiresias, Eurydice

THE DEMANDS ON THE ACTORS

Heracleides, as Creon, has only one part to play, but it is a very long part. He enters early in the play, and is involved in the action until the final scene. Tlepolemos has one long, important woman's role – perhaps Sophocles chose him with this in mind. He also has to deliver two important messenger speeches. Although Haimon and Antigone are to marry, they never appear on stage at the same time, so the same actor can play both parts. Dicaiarchos has several quick changes of character. At one moment he is a princess, then a guard. Later he becomes an old prophet, and finally he is the queen of Thebes. Perhaps on the night before the performance, while Heracleides and Tlepolemos are going over their big speeches to make sure of their words, Dicaiarchos is trying out his different costumes and voices. In the performance he will need expert assistance from the back-stage crew, to help him with his rapid changes of costume. A late entry would be disastrous.

The three actors, and the back-stage crew, arrive early on the day of the performance, and enter the stage-building (*skene*) by the back door. The drawing shows the stage-building, where the actors wait for their entries and change costumes and masks. The man who operates the *mechane* (a kind of crane which can raise characters above the level of the stage) is not needed for *Antigone*, but several other plays in the competition require his skill. The other piece of equipment which is shown, the *ekkyklema*, is a trolley which can be wheeled through the central doors. This is used in *Antigone*, and two men are waiting to wheel it into position.

The drawing also shows the three acting levels. The roof of the *skene*, which is reached by steps from inside the building, can represent a palace roof, as in *Agamemnon*, a play by Aeschylus. Or gods can make their appearances from this roof, as if from the heavens.

THE PLAY BEGINS

We are now ready for the start of the play – and so is the audience. From the earliest glimpse of light they have been flocking to the theatre of Dionysus, and are now crammed together in the seating area, looking down at the bare *orchestra*. They are all waiting for the blast of the trumpet which will announce the start of the competition. *Antigone* is the first of the fifteen plays they will see.

The judges are sworn in. Out of sight in the *skene*, Tlepolemos and Dicaiarchos check their costumes for their first entrance. Sophocles and Bion are giving the cast last-minute words of encouragement. They will not stay in the *skene* during the performance. They would only make a fuss if anything went wrong, and besides, it is their only chance to see the play. The musician who accompanies the chorus gently tunes up. He does not want the audience to hear him, but there is so much excited chatter that he need not worry.

The trumpet sounds, and a sudden hush comes over the audience. As they look towards the *skene*, they see the double doors in the centre swing open. A solitary figure in female clothing emerges, then after a short pause another. The first few words tell the audience that the second girl is called Ismene, and soon her sister Antigone is introduced by name. If the audience do not understand the background to the play, they may lose the thread completely. So Antigone tells Ismene why she has brought her outside the palace, putting the audience in the picture at the same time.

Antigone: I have asked you to come outside so that I can tell you something, without anyone overhearing.
Ismene: What is it, Antigone? I see you have bad news for me.
Antigone: Ismene, do you not know that King Creon has given orders for one of our brothers to be buried, and not the other? Eteocles has had a fine funeral, so I hear, but Polynices, so Creon says, must receive neither burial nor mourning. His body must be left unwept, to be a feast for vultures....
Now you must show whether you are really a king's daughter, or not.
Ismene: Antigone, what can I do? How can I help you?...
Antigone: You can help me bury Polynices' corpse.

Sophocles, *Antigone* l. 18–30, 37–40, 43

But Ismene refuses, and Antigone storms back into the palace, angry at her sister's willingness to obey Creon. Ismene follows her, anxious for her sister.

In the *skene*, Tlepolemos and Dicaiarchos prepare for their next entries. Tlepolemos has to wait some time for his second appearance as Antigone, but Dicaiarchos has a difficult change, since he now becomes a down-to-earth peasant soldier. In the opening scene, the two actors have been able to show something of the characters of the sisters. Ismene is timid and obedient to orders; Antigone is defiant, passionate and dominating. The audience now have an idea what the play will be about. Will Antigone really disobey Creon's orders, and what will happen if she does?

THE ENTRY OF THE CHORUS

Once again the *orchestra* is empty, and the palace doors are shut. But now from the right-hand side, out beyond the *skene*, are heard the strange, reedy notes of the musician. Dressed in splendid costume, he leads in the fifteen members of the chorus. With the quiet dignity of leading Theban citizens they walk towards the rising sun, through the *parodos* and into the *orchestra*. They enter in three rows of five. The best performers are nearest the audience, with the next-best group at the back; in between are those who are less experienced, or who are not quite such good dancers or speakers. All turn and face the audience to sing their opening number. They sing in unison, accompanied by the musician. They act out their song with carefully rehearsed movements.

It is an important moment for Bion. A good opening chorus makes a great impact on the audience, and on the judges too. The chorus take particular care over their words, which must rise above the music and be heard throughout the theatre. They sing of the defeat of the invading army led by Polynices, comparing him to an eagle swooping down on the city; they thank Zeus for delivering Thebes from the enemy. Their words give vital information to the audience, but the chorus also provide a pageant of colour, movement and music. It is difficult for us to imagine how the chorus looked and sounded, since there are no records of their dances or music. But to the Greeks they were just as important as the actors. The choral passages were not

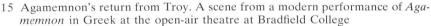

15 Agamemnon's return from Troy. A scene from a modern performance of *Agamemnon* in Greek at the open-air theatre at Bradfield College

merely interludes to separate the acting scenes and give actors time to change their costumes. They made a strong impression of their own. The illustration on page 35, showing the chorus in a modern production, gives an idea of their striking appearance, although it cannot suggest the sound, colour or movement.

THE ENTRY OF CREON

Creon enters (played by Heracleides). The chorus-leader, who is dressed more colourfully than the rest of the chorus, names the new arrival, so that the audience are in no doubt. It is Heracleides' big moment, and he goes straight into a long, important speech, telling the Thebans his decision regarding the brothers.

Creon: I have made the following proclamation about the two sons of Oedipus. Eteocles, who died fighting to defend his city, must receive all the honours due to those who die nobly. The other one (you know who I mean, his brother Polynices), who returned from exile to destroy and set fire to his own land, and turn his people into slaves, must not be buried or mourned by anyone. I forbid it. . . . If I can help it, as long as I live evil will never defeat good. But he who serves his country loyally will be honoured in life and death.

Sophocles, *Antigone*, l. 192–204, 207–10

Heracleides ends his long speech, glad not to have faltered. He has established Creon as a figure of firm authority.

At this moment, from a *parodos*, a soldier enters – one of the men who were guarding Polynices' body on Creon's orders. The actor is Dicaiarchos again, but he now looks and sounds very different from the quiet Ismene. He is a soldier, whose manner and language are rough. But he is also very nervous, and Creon has to order him to come out with his story.

Guard: Well, this is how it is, sir. It's the corpse. Someone's buried it and cleared off, after scattering dust all over the body.
Creon: What do you say? Who has dared do such a thing?
Guard: Don't ask me, sir. There wasn't a trace of a spade or shovel. And as the ground was hard and dry, well, there weren't any tracks, either.

Sophocles, *Antigone*, l. 245–52

The guard finishes his story, insisting that neither he nor his fellow-guards know anything about it. Creon dismisses him angrily, telling him to make sure he finds the culprit, or it will be the worse for him. Then Creon turns and strides back into the palace. The guard hurriedly escapes, relieved to be alive.

THE STORY UNFOLDS

During all this, the chorus have been standing in the *orchestra*, facing the audience. When the guard has left, they sing their next song, a hymn about the achievements of man – suggesting, perhaps, to the minds of the audience the kind of confident, dominating man that Creon is. But they add a comment about death which may hint at the way the play will end.

> In this world are many wonders,
> None more wonderful than man.
> He can sail the stormy ocean;
> Through the deep his way he'll plan.
> Mother earth to him must offer
> Year by year her rich supply.
> As he toils with beasts of burden,
> Nothing can his will deny.
>
> All that lives on earth or heaven,
> All that dwells beneath the sea,
> He can capture with his cunning.
> Nothing from his grasp can flee.
> On the mountainside he chases,
> Hunting lions to their den;
> Horse and cattle learn to heed him.
> All accept the rule of men.
>
> Man has learnt the gift of language;
> Fast as wind his speed of thought.
> Shelters, houses, towns and cities,
> All by man's great skill are wrought.
> His the power that knows no limit;
> His the cure for every ill.
> He has conquered every danger.
> Death alone defeats him still.
> Sophocles, *Antigone*, l. 332–62

After this song, the guard returns. This is a surprise, since he left swearing never to come back. With him, guarded by two soldiers, is Antigone. Most of the audience will have guessed that it was Antigone who covered Polynices' body with dust, but they do not expect her to be caught. She seemed to have got away with it.

16 Antigone, Creon and the guard

Creon is fetched from the palace, and for the first time all three actors are on stage together. A vase-painting (illustration 16) pictures this moment. First, the guard explains, very vividly, why he has returned.

Guard: We swept away the dust from the body, and the corpse lay there again, bare and wet. Then we sat down on the hill, getting as far from the rotting flesh as possible. The smell was terrible. We kept a pretty careful watch, I can tell you. We weren't going to be caught on the hop again. Well, some hours later, with the sun burning down from high in the sky, a duststorm sprang up, swept across the plain, tore the leaves from the trees and filled the sky. The only way to keep the dust out was to shut your eyes tight. Then it stopped, and there she was. It was *her*, right down by the body. She let out a wail, like a mother bird coming home to find her babies all gone from her nest, when she saw that the body was uncovered. Did she curse us! Then, she picks up the dust in her hands, and pours wine from a bronze urn. That did it! We were down there like a shot, and we arrested her. We accused her of covering the body the first time too, and she admitted it.

Well, that puts me in the clear, I'm glad to say, but

I'd rather not have landed her in the cart. I've got nothing against her. But when it's a choice between her and me....

Sophocles, *Antigone*, l. 402–40

The guard has served his purpose, and is dismissed again. There follows an angry scene between Creon and Antigone. For Creon it's simple. The law is the law. For Antigone, it's equally simple. Her brother was her brother, and he had to be buried. That is the law of the dead.

Meanwhile, Dicaiarchos has done another hasty change, and returns as Ismene. Ismene is now ashamed that she did not help Antigone, and claims that she is also guilty. But Antigone refuses her support. It is now too late. Creon, despite his son's intended marriage to Antigone, is determined that she shall die: the law is the law. Antigone and Ismene are taken into the palace, leaving Creon alone with the chorus, who now sing about the disasters which have struck the royal house of Thebes.

Then Haimon enters, giving Tlepolemos his second role. There is a fierce argument between father and son. Haimon says that the people of Thebes do not agree with Creon. Creon replies that he does not take orders from the people of Thebes. He refuses to pardon Antigone, and Haimon departs, very angry. Then Creon announces the fate of Antigone. She is to be walled up in a cave with a little food. Creon believes that he will avoid bringing guilt to the city of Thebes if he does not kill her directly.

Shortly after, Antigone comes from the palace, guarded. She grieves for her fate. She was to have been escorted to her marriage, but instead she is to be led to her funeral. Creon again comes out, but not to pity her. He orders her to be taken at once to her rocky tomb, and Antigone, a sad figure, disappears through the *parodos*.

THE CLIMAX APPROACHES

The mood of the chorus is now very different. Their next dance is slower, and the music is sad. Creon still stands there. In talking to Antigone and Haimon he has shown no pity. But now he has another test. This time he must face Teiresias, an old, blind prophet much respected by the people of Thebes. He enters, led by a boy, and the slow pace of Antigone's farewell is echoed by his gradual progress across the theatre. The boy is an 'extra', with no words to speak. But it is a big day for him too. Who knows? In a few years' time he may be an actor like Dicaiarchos. So he listens and watches carefully as the experienced actor now adopts the movements and speech of an old man – though not a weak old man: he is a powerful threat to Creon.

Creon greets Teiresias respectfully, and listens to his words. They

17 Creon (kneeling) and the blind prophet Teiresias (from a production at Whitgift School)

are not pleasant. The prophet claims that it is Creon's fault that his sacrifices have not been accepted by the gods. But Creon still refuses to change his mind; he thinks Teiresias is trying to deceive him, perhaps for money. After angry exchanges (see illustration 17), Teiresias is led away by the boy. His parting words warn Creon that his own son Haimon will die.

Creon is worried, and he discusses with the chorus-leader what he should do. Finally, he accepts the advice that he should release Antigone, and hurries away. The chorus now sing a very joyful song, a hymn to Dionysus, god of revelry and the theatre. The scene might well seem set for a happy ending. But then a messenger enters, from the *parodos* by which Antigone and Creon both left.

THE MESSENGER-SPEECH

No murder or violent action could take place on stage in Greek tragedy. The theatre was sacred to Dionysus, and violent death polluted holy ground. So everything had to be conveyed to the audience in words, by a messenger who gave an eye-witness account. Such messenger-speeches are often among the most vivid moments in a play, and affected the audience far more than if the deaths were shown on stage. To deliver a messenger-speech called for the actor's greatest skill, and in *Antigone* Tlepolemos has to give two. He has just recovered from the difficult role of Antigone, using a strong female voice. Now he is a man again, and he summons all his vocal powers for the speech. First he builds the suspense, describing the scene as Creon, accompanied by some of his servants, approaches the rocky hill. Then he comes to his climax. Creon, he says, has just heard a sound from inside the cave, and is convinced that it is Haimon.

Messenger: There, right in the farthest corner of the cave, we saw her, hanging dead from a noose made by her own clothing. And there was Haimon, grieving for his dead bride, and for his father's cruelty. Creon rushed to him, crying:
'Poor boy, what have you done? Why have you come here? I beg you, come away from this place. Come with me.'
But Haimon's eyes flashed with hatred, and he spat, full in his father's face. Then he drew a sword and struck. Creon dodged the blow and fled, while Haimon, in a frenzy, thrust the sword deep in his own side. As the blood gushed from his mouth, he gave Antigone a final kiss, and the blood stained her white cheeks red.
And so they lie, wedded in death, their bodies united.
Sophocles, *Antigone*, l. 1220–40

Eurydice, the queen, has listened in silence, but before the end of the speech she goes into the palace. The messenger hurries after her, and at this moment a sad procession appears from the *parodos*. Creon is leading the body of Haimon, borne by the servants, back home. At last he has learnt wisdom, but too late. 'The gods have destroyed my happiness', he says.

But the final blow has still to fall. The messenger comes from the palace, and delivers his second speech. Eurydice has taken her own life. The central doors are flung open, and her body is brought out on the *ekkyklema* (a wheeled trolley often used for such moments – see the illustration on page 32). Creon can bear no more. He asks the gods to kill him too, but his punishment is to remain alive. Slaves lead him away, a broken man. The audience is completely silent. In the *orchestra* stand the chorus, where they have been since their first entry. Now they turn quietly and leave. The final, brief words of the play, which they chant, sum up the play's message.

The greatest part of happiness is wisdom;
Divine laws man ought always to uphold.
To boastful tongues sure punishment will follow,
And wisdom we learn only when we're old.
Sophocles, *Antigone*, l. 1347–53

THE PLAY'S EFFECT

The effect on the audience can be imagined. They have followed with intense emotion the moods of the actors and chorus. They have wept and suffered with Antigone; her death (and the deaths of Haimon and Eurydice) has affected them deeply. But the final sight is the ruined Creon, and they feel sympathy even for him, despite his earlier pride and cruelty.

A hundred years after *Antigone* was first performed, the writer Aristotle used the word *catharsis* to describe the effect of tragedies. The word means 'cleansing', as though the feelings the audience had experienced – fear, joy, pity, suspense – had been washed out of them. Sometimes people say that a play has left them 'drained'. This may be a little like the state of the audience when *Antigone* ended, but there was more to it than that. Watching the play was a religious experience for the Greeks. They were not mere spectators, but involved themselves deeply in the play. At the end came a release of all the tension and passion. There was exhilaration as well as exhaustion.

Perhaps the most amazing thing is that after *Antigone*, with only a short pause, actors, chorus and audience began a second tragedy, followed by a third. Only then did the deep feelings give way to the lighter mood of the satyr-play and comedy.

THE THEME OF 'ANTIGONE'

Antigone is not simply a theatrical experience. Sophocles meant his audience to think, and the questions he raised are still important today. Should the law of the land always be obeyed? How should someone act when his conscience clashes with the law? What should the state do with such a person? Is a king like Creon wrong to think he must stand by his decisions? Or is he wrong only when he ignores advice or treats people with arrogance, as Creon treated Antigone, Haimon and particularly Teiresias? Such questions are still discussed today, and the discussions cannot be very different from the arguments that went on in Athens at the time when Sophocles wrote *Antigone*.

A FOOTNOTE ON GREEK TRAGEDY

Not all Greek tragedies were like *Antigone*. Within a basic pattern, there were great variations. Of the many hundreds that were written, thirty-two survive today. Appendix B (page 73) gives the complete list.

4 Comedy in Greece

THE LENAIA

We will now leave Greek tragedy and turn to comedy, and we move to another festival of Dionysus, the Lenaia. This was a winter festival, held in January and only attended by Athenians, because the seas were too stormy to be safe for travel. As at the Great Dionysia, there were tragedies and comedies, but no satyr-plays. Comedy was more important than tragedy at the Lenaia. The great tragic playwrights rarely presented plays at this festival, where only two tragic writers competed, each with two plays. Five comic playwrights had their opportunity (except for a period late in the fifth century BC when the war between Athens and Sparta reduced the number to three), each with a single play. As at the Great Dionysia, there were prizes for the best writer and actor in tragedy and in comedy.

The Lenaia took its name from *lenai*, another name given to the female worshippers of Dionysus, who are shown celebrating this festival in the vase-painting below.

18 Dionysus and worshippers at the Lenaia, another festival of Dionysus

AN ACTOR PREPARES FOR THE LENAIA

The Lenaia is described in *The Mask of Apollo*, a novel by Mary Renault about the life of a Greek actor. In the following extract, a tragic actor tells how he prepares to take part.

On the eve of the festival I lay listening to the noise of the midnight rites; the cries of the women trying, as they ran about the streets, to sound like *maenads* on a mountain. Their hymns, and their squeals of 'Iakchos' and the red light of torches sliding across my ceiling, would wake me whenever my eyes had closed. Towards morning, I heard a huddle of them go by with their torches out, shivering and grumbling, and complaining of the rain.

Next day opened cloudy, not the rank bad weather that gets the show put off, but grey and threatening. During the first of the comedies it looked so black that the people stayed at home, and the theatre was half empty; if the cast had been less discouraged, I think the play might have won. . . .

On the day when the contest of the tragedies started, the wind got up. The audience came muffled to the eyes, their cloaks pulled over their heads, and with two cloaks if they had them. . . .

The following day was ours.

I could not sleep. I thought of taking poppy-syrup; but it leaves one dull, and one would do better tired. . . . I tossed and turned, and put my hand to the window, and felt the air still, but very cold. . . . Suddenly I woke to daybreak. The lamp had burned out; birds were chirping. The sky was clear. . . .

When we got to the theatre, the public benches were full of people bundled up in all they had, with hats pulled down on their ears. Down below, in the seats of honour, ambassadors and *archons* [officials], priests and *choregoi* with their guests were coming in, their slaves all laden with rugs and cushions to make them snug. Then came the greater priests and priestesses. Presently drums and cymbals sounded; the image of Dionysus was carried in and set down facing the *orchestra*, where he could see his servants play; his High Priest took the central throne; the trumpet sounded, and ceased. . . .

M. Renault, The Mask of Apollo

ARISTOPHANES AND OLD COMEDY

The only surviving examples of Old Comedy – that is, the comedies of the fifth century BC – were written by Aristophanes. (See Appendix B.) We have eleven of his plays, and there are fragments or records of another thirty-two. Aristophanes was evidently the most successful comic writer of his time. But he did not always win first prize, and it is a pity that no other comedies survive to make it possible for us to compare him with his rivals.

Aristophanes sometimes presented his plays at the Great Dionysia, and sometimes at the Lenaia. Perhaps he was more successful at the Lenaia, where, with no foreigners present, he had greater freedom to put forward his ideas – which often criticised politicians of the day.

His writing career stretched over forty years, starting in 427 BC. For most of this time Athens was engaged in a bitter war with its rival city–state Sparta, so that many of his plays were written and performed in wartime. But fighting did not normally take place during the winter months, and the Lenaia was held at a quiet time of the year. Aristophanes' plays usually took their titles from the chorus, and the titles show what a variety of costumes the comic choruses wore: *The Birds*, *The Knights*, *The Frogs*, *The Clouds*, *The Wasps*. You have already seen the kind of costume worn for *The Birds* (page 10), and the vase-painting on this page shows a chorus of horsemen like the chorus in *The Knights*.

19 A chorus of horsemen

ACTING IN OLD COMEDY

There were similarities between acting in tragedy and in comedy. In each there were only three actors, who often had to play several parts, though this rule was not applied quite so strictly in comedy, and 'extras' could play minor speaking parts. Comic actors also wore special costumes and masks, and they relied greatly on the audience's powers of imagination: the same simple theatre, with few props and little scenery, served for both tragedy and comedy.

But there were differences. Actors who have to try to make audiences laugh need to have a special ability to win them over. But if they work too hard at it, they overact and become less funny, not more. Today, producers of comedy on television practically tell audiences when to laugh, by playing recorded laughter at the right moment. And studio audiences are prompted by flashing lights: *applaud*, *laugh*. But in the theatre there are no automatic laughs, and comic actors learn to their cost how differently audiences react.

It must have been particularly difficult for Aristophanes and his rivals. Their plays were presented to a cold, sometimes wet audience sitting in the open air on a wintry day. However funny the play was, everything depended on how well the actors could put the humour across to the audience.

COMIC COSTUMES

The costumes worn in comedy were quite different from those worn in tragedy. Male characters generally had a short tunic and cloak, coming down not much below the waist, with thick tights covering their legs. The costumes were padded in front and behind to make the actors look short and fat. There were many variations from the basic costume. Actors representing female characters would be dressed accordingly, and there were special costumes for more unusual characters, which added to the colour and variety. Some idea of the appearance of comic actors is given by illustrations of comedies which were performed in Italy (see the vase-painting below).

The masks had exaggerated expressions, and large mouths. Sometimes portrait-masks, with any prominent feature enlarged as in a

20 Comic actors

cartoon caricature, represented real Athenians. The comedies often made fun of important citizens.

Another essential piece of equipment was the *phallos*. This is perhaps the most surprising item to us today, and to many people the most shocking. It was a large leather construction strapped to the waist, in the shape of a man's penis, but very much exaggerated in size. It was worn either tied up, so that it was not too obvious, or untied if there were jokes about it, as there often were. For example, in Aristophanes' play *Women at the Thesmophoria*, a man disguises himself in women's clothes and attends the *Thesmophoria*, a festival to which only women were admitted. The women are warned that a man is present, and to prove it the man has to be stripped by the women. He tries desperately to keep the *phallos* hidden from them, but eventually of course they spot it, in a scene causing great merriment.

The *phallos* was associated with the worship of Dionysus. For the Greeks, it was a powerful symbol of fertility, standing for life and fruitfulness. It was not considered obscene or shocking. Some people may not have liked the jokes about the *phallos*, but if they did not, presumably they did not go to the theatre to watch comedy. Some modern translations of Aristophanes' plays leave out references to the *phallos*. Aristophanes' comedies are often considered too shocking to stage in their original form, even in these permissive times.

THE PLAYS

As with tragedy, you cannot get a real idea of what Greek comedy was like by reading books. Comic effects depend so much on what is seen that it is important to watch or act performances of them. But if we take a short summary of one of Aristophanes' plays, we may be able to find out something about how his comedy got its laughs.

'THE CLOUDS'

Today *The Clouds* is one of Aristophanes' best-known plays, but it was not a success when it was first produced. It came last in the competition, and Aristophanes was so disappointed that he rewrote it. This revised version, which we have today, may not have been performed in Aristophanes' lifetime.

An old Athenian citizen, Strepsiades, has got into debt through his son's extravagance. The son, Pheidippides, takes after his mother, who comes from a wealthy family. He is mad about horses – still an expensive hobby. To get out of debt, Strepsiades wants Pheidippides to go to the 'Thinkshop', where Socrates the philosopher teaches students how to make an 'Unfair Argument' defeat a 'Fair Argument'. Pheidippides refuses, so Strepsiades decides to go himself. But he is old and slow, and Socrates finds it difficult to teach him anything. While he is trying, the Clouds watch, and give Strepsiades encouragement. They are the chorus, and they stand for the vague, woolly nature of Socrates' wisdom, as Aristophanes presents it. They are supposed to be the new goddesses in whom Socrates and his students believe (they have got rid of Zeus and the other old gods). Eventually Socrates introduces two characters who represent the Fair and Unfair Arguments. They have a contest which the Unfair Argument wins, after a heated debate. Strepsiades now feels ready to meet the people he owes money to, and he drives them away with what he imagines are examples of the Unfair Argument. He also demonstrates this to Pheidippides, but Pheidippides learns the lesson too well, and he proves that it is right for him to beat Strepsiades, in return for thrashings he received as a boy. So he starts to thrash his father, and this causes Strepsiades finally to abandon the Unfair Argument. The play ends as Strepsiades takes his revenge on Socrates by trying to destroy the 'Thinkshop' and angrily chasing Socrates' students away.

HUMOUR IN ARISTOPHANES

The above summary gives some idea of the antics which might go on in a Greek comedy. We are now going to look more closely at some of the comic effects which Aristophanes uses.

Satire

In satire, people (or their ideas) are made to look ridiculous, often in order to make other people distrust them. Politicians are a favourite target for satire, as in several of Aristophanes' plays. *The Clouds* is a satire on Socrates and the philosophers known as Sophists. Aristophanes is making fun of the new ideas which people were putting forward, some of which he believed were dangerous.

Impersonation

Satire often involves impersonating the person being attacked, and the actor playing Socrates probably imitated the movements, appearance and voice of the real Socrates. There is a story that Socrates was present at the first performance of *The Clouds*, and that he stood up during the play to let himself be seen – perhaps to show what a good likeness it was. Some modern comedians are impersonators, but unlike the satirists, they are not usually trying to influence audiences' opinions. Politicians might well object to impersonations if they thought people would take them seriously. As it is, they seem to enjoy being impersonated. Perhaps they are pleased to get the publicity.

Visual humour

Some things are funny just because they look funny. As the old silent films show, visual humour can be of many kinds. The most obvious sort is 'knockabout' – throwing custard pies, slipping on banana skins, and mock violence. In *The Clouds*, when Socrates first appears he is swung in front of the *skene* by means of the *mechane*, a crane used for special effects (see illustration 14 on page 32), sitting in a large basket which is suspended high above the ground. When Strepsiades asks why he is in the basket, he explains that it helps him to think higher thoughts.

Verbal humour
Jokes, puns and funny stories rely on what is said, not what is seen. Aristophanes was particularly fond of puns (playing on words). Many comedians use them today, probably expecting a groan rather than a laugh. Since Aristophanes' plays were in Greek, it is hard to appreciate his puns today. At the beginning of *The Clouds*, Socrates' students are trying to discover how a gnat sings – through its mouth or through its bottom. (This is meant to show what a waste of time their studies are.) They decide that the sound comes from the bottom, and there is a pun on the Greek words for 'investigation' and 'bottom', which are similar. Several translators have tried to get this over in English. They call the study an 'intestigation', or 'anal analysis', or an inquiry into 'a gnat's agnatomy'.

Topical allusions
Jokes are often about something which is in the news. In 1976, comedy was full of jokes about inflation and the drought. Such humour stops being funny very quickly, since it has to be right up to date. Aristophanes' allusions to people or events of nearly 2,500 years ago do not seem funny now, and modern versions of his plays often leave them out or try to update them.

Sex and religion
Some subjects are regarded as 'taboo' – that is, they are not supposed to be made fun of or discussed in polite company. In many societies two such subjects are sex and religion, which for the Greeks were very closely connected. They worshipped Dionysus as a god of fertility. Today many jokes involve a mixture of sex and religion, and both subjects are extremely common in comedy shows. *The Clouds* has some sexual humour, though not as much as some of Aristophanes' other plays. There is also a good deal of joking about religion, since Aristophanes wanted to make fun of some religious ideas. Socrates has invented new gods, he says, with strange names like 'Air' and 'Chaos'.

Situation comedy
A common form of comedy is what we call 'situation comedy'. The

characters are ordinary people, who act in rather unusual ways when facing the situations and problems of daily life. Situation comedy can include all the above types of humour and many others. We laugh at the characters partly because they are like ourselves, and their problems are often ours. But we also laugh because they cannot cope with the problems. We often know what they should do, and so we feel superior to them. Aristophanes' plays contain many elements like those in situation comedy. In *The Clouds*, we can all understand the plight of a father who has got into debt through his son's expensive hobbies, and we can laugh at Strepsiades' stupidity when he tries to learn philosophy.

21 A scene from a recent modern production of *The Clouds* at King's College, London. Pheidippides, who is mad about horses, is dressed in a jockey's outfit. In the background is a member of the Chorus of Clouds

PLAYS ABOUT THE WAR

The war between Athens and Sparta dragged on for twenty-seven years, and three of Aristophanes' plays are concerned with attempts to make peace. In *The Acharnians*, an Athenian citizen makes a private peace treaty with the Spartans, and other Athenians envy his good fortune. In *Peace*, the hero, Trygaios, fattens up a giant dung-beetle to take him to heaven to rescue the goddess Peace, who has been locked away by War. The scene when the *mechane* hoists Trygaios above the stage-building on his beetle, called Pegasus, is a fine piece of visual humour (see illustration 14 on page 32). The third play about the war is *Lysistrata*. This time it is the women who want peace. Lysistrata, an Athenian woman, summons women from Sparta and other Greek cities, and persuades them not to make love to their husbands until the men promise to vote for peace. As the play proceeds, the men grow increasingly desperate, while the women still refuse to give in to them. Finally the men were forced to agree to their demands, and the war is ended. *Lysistrata* was written late in the war, when things were going badly for the Athenians, and Aristophanes must have voiced a common desire for peace in this play. But what gives the comedy its originality and humour is the very idea of a general 'sex-strike'; this is funny in itself, and leads to hilarious consequences.

SATIRICAL PLAYS

The Clouds makes fun of Socrates, but Aristophanes also had other targets. One of these is the tragic playwright Euripides, who features in several plays. Sometimes Aristophanes includes extracts from his plays, in comic situations, or imitates his tragic style – a form of comedy known as parody. Some of the audience must have known Euripides' plays very well, or the point of the parody would have been lost.

Parody is found in *The Frogs*, a play which takes its name from the chorus of frogs whose song accompanies the god Dionysus across the Styx (the lake which leads to Hades, the underworld). Dionysus wishes to bring back a dead playwright, because the new tragic writers are not good enough for his Festivals. (Sophocles and Euripides had both died shortly before the play was written, and Aeschylus was also dead.) In the play there is a competition between Aeschylus and Euripides, to see who is the better playwright and should return to earth. Aeschylus wins, as his criticisms of Euripides' style are more effective than Euripides' attack on the long words that Aeschylus uses.

Euripides features in other plays, but the satire is not usually very bitter. Aristophanes kept most of his bitterness for Cleon, a leading politician of the time, who was opposed to peace. There are a number of sneers at the fact that Cleon owned a factory, and therefore came from a rather low-class family by Aristophanes' standards. The attacks are often savage, and no doubt they seemed very funny to Cleon's opponents. But Cleon was not amused, and once he was so angry that he summoned Aristophanes to appear before the Council. However, the attacks continued, and the Athenians tolerated them. It is interesting to compare the freedom of speech Aristophanes enjoyed with what our comedians are allowed to say. What would happen if politicians today were violently abused, or accused of immoral behaviour and swindling the people? And what would have happened during the Second World War if a comic playwright had made jokes attacking Churchill's military strategy, and accusing the British of being partly to blame for the war? Yet this was exactly the sort of thing that Aristophanes did in Athens.

ACTING THE PLAYS

Even now we have only had a glimpse of the range of Aristophanes' humour. Fortunately there are many good translations of the plays, though sometimes the humour is lost in English. However, comedies by Aristophanes can still appeal to modern audiences, and some of them are performed quite often. Perhaps you will have a chance to see a performance, and then you will be able to judge the plays more easily. Acting them yourselves is an even better way of getting to know them.

FROM OLD TO NEW COMEDY

In *The Frogs*, Dionysus visited the underworld hoping to bring back a dead playwright. But this was impossible even for a god. The great tragic playwrights were gone for ever. The year after *The Frogs* was performed, 404 BC, Athens lost the war. Although Aristophanes carried on writing for some years, his plays started to change in style. We refer to his last plays as *Middle Comedy*, to distinguish them from the *Old Comedy* we have so far been considering. They had lost the political satire and the lively, farcical quality of the earlier plays. With Aristophanes' death, the great period in Greek playwriting came to an end. We only have small fragments of the works of the hundreds of comic writers who were active in the fifty years following his death. By the time we reach Menander, the only other Greek comic playwright whose works survive, more changes had taken place. We call this last period of comedy *New Comedy*.

CHANGES IN THE THEATRE

Another thing that had changed was the appearance of the theatres. From the fourth century BC, magnificent stone theatres were built all

22 The theatre at Epidauros

over Greece, and also in Italy, Sicily and parts of Asia Minor (modern Turkey). One outstanding example is the theatre at Epidauros, in southern Greece (illustration 22). Today the stage-buildings, made of stone, have been almost destroyed, but the seating-area is much as it was when it was first constructed. As the theatres developed, the stage (formerly a low wooden platform) became a four-metre high stone construction, on which all the action took place. This made the *orchestra* less important, and the original circle was reduced to a semi-circle. This can be seen in the theatre of Dionysus as it is today (page 27), and also in the theatre at Delphi which is shown below.

23 The theatre at Delphi

The great festivals of Athens were still the centre of dramatic activity, but now professional touring companies took the plays all round Greece and to Italy and Asia Minor. The acting profession began to flourish, and soon actors formed themselves into a union, called The Servants of Dionysus. In many ways the Greek theatre was still thriving, but there were no playwrights to match those of the fifth century BC. The theatre began to rely much more on revivals of the earlier plays, especially those of Aeschylus, Sophocles and Euripides. Euripides, though less popular than the other two in his lifetime, now became the firm favourite – perhaps because his plays seemed more 'modern' in their ideas – with the result that eighteen of his tragedies have survived, more than the total number of plays by Sophocles and Aeschylus (seven each).

MENANDER

Our last Greek playwright, Menander, wrote his first play in 321 BC. When he died (about 290 BC) he had written over a hundred comedies, for country festivals and performances abroad as well as for the Great Dionysia. In Athens he was not particularly successful. He won the first prize only eight times, and two years running came fifth and last. Until recently, his plays had almost completely disappeared, but

24   Menander studying masks for a play. The wide-open mouth and wrinkled forehead are typical features of the comic masks

an ancient papyrus-roll was found which contained the text of one whole play (*The Bad-Tempered Man*) and large portions of several others. Menander was greatly admired by Roman playwrights, who often translated his plays into Latin. The picture shows Menander in his room, studying possible masks for his characters (illustration 24).

The plays of Menander and other writers of *New Comedy* abandoned the greatly exaggerated costumes of Aristophanes' day. Ordinary clothes were adopted, though the mask was still worn. Menander's plays are about ordinary people, with themes which affect all people of all ages: money, romance, bringing up children. The characters were often realistic; they did not act in silly ways all the time. The chorus was no longer important, and Menander's scripts did not include words for their musical interludes. Many people consider that Menander was a very fine writer, but it is hard for us to judge. Only *The Bad-Tempered Man* is complete enough to be acted, and performances are very rare. However, as we can study the plays of the Roman comic writers he influenced so much, we will now leave Greece, and turn our attention to Italy.

5 Comedy in Rome

EARLY ITALIAN PLAYS

During the fifth and fourth centuries BC, when Greek drama was at its height, the city of Rome was gradually increasing its power over neighbouring peoples, and by the third century the Romans controlled all Italy. They took over many ideas from the other people who lived in Italy, as well as from the Greeks (who had founded settlements in various parts of the country). Even before the Romans became powerful, there was much theatrical activity in Italy.

One popular kind of entertainment was known as the *phlyax*-play, from a Greek word meaning 'gossip'. *Phlyax*-plays were comical in style, using Greek legends, but changing the stories in humorous ways. There are scenes from the plays on many vase-paintings. One of

25 Jupiter and Alcmena

these (illustration 25) portrays Jupiter's affair with a mortal woman, Alcmena, whom he deceived by disguising himself as her husband, Amphitryo. Alcmena is looking down from a window, while the god Mercury assists Jupiter by holding out a lamp for him to see where to put his ladder.

The second example is also a scene from a play. What can you work out from this picture? (The scene is explained in the Further Study section at the end of the book, but see what you can discover without looking this up.)

Another kind of dramatic entertainment was the farcical plays known as the Atellan plays (from the name of a town in southern Italy). At first these were improvised – that is, made up on the spot. Later, as their popularity spread, they had written scripts. They contained a few popular characters, who appeared regularly; we call these *stock characters*. There was *Pappus* (the grandfather); *Maccus* and *Bucco* (two fools); and *Manducus* (a greedy ogre with great chewing jaws, which could be shown clearly on the masks).

26 Scene from a comedy

There was also the *mime*, usually presented by a single actor accompanied on the pipes. Mime relies on gesture and facial expression to tell a story, and is a very skilled form of acting. A famous modern French mime artist is Marcel Marceau.

ROMAN COMEDY

These popular shows went into the making of Roman comedy, but the main ingredient was Greek *New Comedy*. All the plays by the two Roman comic playwrights whose works survive (Plautus and Terence) are translations or adaptations of plays by Menander and his rival playwrights. We cannot tell exactly how much the Roman writers changed the original plays, but they could, to some extent, adapt the plots, introduce topical jokes or puns in Latin, and alter characters.

THE THEATRE IN THE TIME OF PLAUTUS

Despite the fact that the Greeks had built splendid stone theatres, some of them in Italy, the city of Rome had no permanent theatre at the time of Plautus (who lived from about 240 to 180 BC). Temporary wooden buildings were constructed for the performances which were held, like Greek productions, at festivals in honour of the gods. For his plays Plautus needed a long wooden stage to represent a street, and a building behind the stage, which usually showed the fronts of three houses. At each end of the stage there was a side entrance – one used by people arriving from nearby, and one for long-distance travellers. The doors into the houses were used throughout the plays, since all action had to take place in the street. There was little scenery. Because the plays were originally Greek, the scene was usually meant to be Athens or some other part of Greece.

THE AUDIENCE

The playwrights often had a hard time with Roman audiences. At the festivals, various other entertainments also took place. The audience was a mixture of citizens and slaves, women and children, and if a popular attraction turned up at the moment when your play was about to begin, there was nothing you could do about it. For the Romans, festivals were holidays much more as we think of them. People wanted to be amused, and playwrights had to take their chance with jugglers, acrobats, boxers and the rest.

THE ACTORS

The position of actors had also changed. In Athens, the winning *protagonist* was something of a national hero. But the Romans generally had little respect for the acting profession. Their word for a company of actors was *grex*, which also means a flock of sheep. Many actors were slaves, or came from the lower classes of citizens. Another change was that the chorus had now completely disappeared. There were only the actors.

THE PRODUCER

The production was in the hands of the *dominus gregis* or 'master of the flock', who was also usually the chief actor. One of these was Turpio, who produced all Terence's plays. He made a contract with the magistrate in charge of the festival, hired the actors and arranged rehearsals. It was also his duty to provide a musician for the accompaniment – for music continued to provide a background to parts of the plays, despite the disappearance of the chorus. Before the production, the playwright sold the play either to the producer or to the festival official. It was then out of his control. He received no more money after a successful performance, or if the play was repeated. But if it was a disaster, the playwright ran no risks – it was the producer who stood to lose. So at the start of the play, as leading actor, he tried to catch the attention of the fickle audience, and sometimes made almost desperate appeals to them to treat the play kindly. The producer had absolute control over the company. In one play, the producer tells the audience, in an aside, that after the performance 'the actors will take their costumes off, and any actors who have made a mistake will get a beating'.

COSTUMES

The basic garment was the tunic, a linen or woollen shirt with holes for the neck and arms. It was pulled on over the head, and could be tied with a girdle. Sometimes it was worn by itself, but more often under a woollen wrap. The actors wore light sandals and, especially if they were travellers, sometimes had a hat. Actors portraying women were dressed very similarly. These were the clothes worn by ordinary Greeks, and since the plays came from Greece, the costume was kept. Different characters wore various colours: the rich wore purple, prostitutes yellow.

The masks also gave the audience an idea of what kind of character to expect. One ancient writer lists forty-four types of mask worn in comedy: eleven for young men, seven for slaves (red-haired, as a rule), three for old women, five for young women, seven for prostitutes, two for slave-girls, and a few others. What type do you think the mask on page 60 is? Some characters could also be recognised from their 'props'. Soldiers regularly carried swords, and cooks had a

27 A comic mask

kitchen knife or spoon. Actors still changed from one part to another, as in the Greek theatre, but this was not so common, since there was no longer any need to use only three actors.

PLAUTUS

Plautus was the earlier of the two Roman comic playwrights whose plays still exist. His twenty-one surviving plays make him the best-known of all the ancient playwrights. We cannot deal with all his plays, but here is the plot of one of the most famous.

'THE GHOST-STORY' (MOSTELLARIA)

Theopropides, an old Athenian gentleman, has been abroad on business for three years. In his absence his son, a young man called Philolaches, lives a wild life with wine, women and song. A cunning slave, Tranio, has helped Philolaches to free his latest girl-friend, Philematium, from slavery but he has had to borrow from a money-lender.

Early in the play there is a merry drinking-party with Philolaches, Philematium and some friends, including the very drunk Callidamates. Suddenly Tranio arrives with the alarming news that Theopropides is on his way home from the harbour. The banqueters panic, but Tranio bundles them all inside, telling them to keep completely silent. When the old man arrives, Tranio invents a story: the house is haunted by a ghost, and is now deserted. There are awkward noises from inside, but Tranio convinces Theopropides that the ghost is angry, and that he ought to flee. Just then the money-lender arrives, demanding his money. Tranio produces more lies, saying that Philolaches has had to borrow money to buy a house – the house next door, in fact. Theopropides is about to inspect the house, to see if it is worth buying, when the owner (inevitably) comes home. Tranio's stories become wilder and wilder, and everyone is totally confused. Eventually Theopropides discovers that Tranio has been lying, and threatens to kill him. Tranio flees to the altar for protection. But Callidamates, now sober, persuades the old man to treat everything as a joke, settles up, and the play ends happily after all.

PLAUTUS' COMEDY

The Ghost-Story is typical of Plautus and *New Comedy* in several ways. Some *stock characters* are always turning up. There are the old father and the wild son, shown here in the lively painting of a *phlyax*-play (illustration 28); and there is the cunning slave, a very popular character. But Plautus (or perhaps Philemon, who wrote the Greek original) has turned stock characters into individuals, especially Tranio, one of the best examples of his type. The play relies greatly on visual humour, at which Plautus was a master. An obvious example is the arrival of the drunken Callidamates. He cannot stand up properly, stammers over his words and does not know where he is. The complicated plot, with all the confusion, is also a source of much fun.

Most of Plautus' plays have complicated plots, involving misunderstandings, mistakes or deception. In *The Pot of Gold* (*Aulularia*), there is a mean old man who thinks that a young man has stolen his gold, when in fact he has stolen his daughter. The old man is greatly relieved when he finds that the young man is only interested in stealing her, and not the gold. In *The Menaechmi*, twin brothers are reunited after a series of misunderstandings; both have been in the same town, without realising that the other is there, so there are many cases of mistaken identity. Similar confusion is caused in *Amphitryo* (the story illustrated on page 56); when Jupiter disguises himself as Amphitryo to deceive Alcmena, Amphitryo's wife. Neither the husband nor the wife can work out what happened.

Mistakes like this are often caused by trickery, like that of Tranio in *The Ghost-Story*. In *The Swaggering Soldier* (*Miles Gloriosus*), the

28 An old man escorts his drunken son home from a late-night party. The old man
(on the right) is looking round anxiously (or angrily?) to see if his son can still
walk. The young man has a tambourine in one hand and an oil-lamp in the other.
He is wearing a garland on his head, showing that he has been celebrating. He is
only just managing to keep his balance

'hero' has the splendid name Pyrgopolynices – Plautus, like many
other comic writers, loved long, amusing names. Pyrgopolynices
thinks he is a real ladykiller, and is deceived by the wily Palaestrio into
thinking that a girl is madly in love with him. But Palaestrio has also
been arranging for the girl to meet her real lover through a hole which
has been knocked in the wall between two houses. Pyrgopolynices is
made to look a complete fool, and the play ends with him thanking his
lucky stars that he did not get into any worse trouble for trying to
seduce the girl.

There is trickery and confusion in many modern comedies. Either by accident or because they are deceived, people get into impossible situations, and have somehow or other to escape. The plays of the French farce writer Feydeau, or the Whitehall farces of Brian Rix, are full of such situations, but they are also found in many other types of comedy. Or a man may be accused by a policeman of being a burglar when he is trying to enter his own house after losing his key. You can probably think of many other examples – what impossible situations have you enjoyed in television comedies?

TERENCE

Many similar kinds of humour are found in Terence, who was born at about the time when Plautus died. He came from Africa as a slave, but was freed. He started producing plays when he was only about eighteen, but his career was a short one; his last play, *The Brothers* (*Adelphi*), was written only six years later. *The Mother-in-Law* (*Hecyra*) was produced three times, because the first two performances were total failures. Terence suffered from the conditions in which Roman comedies were produced. The prologue to the third performance, delivered as usual by his producer Turpio, explains the problem:

> Once again I bring you *The Mother-in-Law*. I have never been allowed to present this play in silence; it has been overwhelmed by disasters. If you show your appreciation of our efforts this time, we will undo the damage. The first time I began to act, there was a rumour that some famous boxers, and perhaps a tight-rope walker too, were arriving. Friends started talking to each other, and the women were shouting – so I made a premature exit. . . . Well, I tried again, and everyone enjoyed the opening. But then someone said that there were gladiators on the programme, and people started flooding in, rioting and fighting for seats, with an almighty din. That was the end of *my* little performance.
>
> Terence, *Hecyra* (the prologue)

But in spite of these difficulties, Terence continued to write. He was more serious than Plautus, and less prepared to give the audiences obvious things to laugh at. He believed, as Aristophanes and Menander had done, that a comic playwright ought to have something to teach his audience, and his ideas had a great influence on later writers. This is why we still have his six plays. If he had lived longer, there would have been many more. But he died soon after the performance of *The Brothers*, aged about twenty-five. He is supposed to have died while he was on a journey to Greece – perhaps to get some more plays to adapt for the Roman stage. So far as Roman comedy is concerned, his death definitely marks the end of a chapter.

6   The End of an Era?

TRAGEDY IN ROME

As well as the comedies described in the last chapter, Roman audiences watched tragedies by Roman writers such as Ennius, Pacuvius and Accius. Their plays, from the third century BC, were performed for more than two hundred years, and crowds knew parts of them so well that it was said that once when an actor missed his cue, twelve hundred voices chorused the words. But apart from a few fragments, these plays, modelled closely on Greek tragedy, have all disappeared. However, Roman art has many illustrations of tragic actors, such as the striking painting from Pompeii of an actor preparing to put on a mask (see below).

29   A tragic actor with his mask

Roman tragic masks always had the *onkos*, a raised hairstyle similar to that worn by Roman ladies. This *onkos*, and also the high platform shoes which were introduced, made actors look taller, standing out clearly on the high stone stages. It is interesting to compare this picture with the much earlier vase-painting which shows a Greek actor studying his mask (on page 24). Some more Roman masks are shown below.

30 Roman masks

THE THEATRE AND THE EMPERORS

In 27 BC, Augustus became the first emperor in Rome. The Republic, which produced the comic and tragic playwrights mentioned above, had ended after Julius Caesar's assassination in 44 BC. Apart from occasional revivals, their plays were seen no more. But the temporary wooden theatres of Plautus and Terence were replaced by grand stone buildings. The first permanent theatre in Rome was the theatre of Pompey, built in 55 BC. During the next century similar theatres spread throughout the Roman Empire. These were in the style of the Greek theatres, but they also had fine decorations in the Roman style. Behind the stage, the buildings which formed the background became showpieces of Roman architecture. A good example of a Roman theatre which is still in use is the theatre of Herodes Atticus at Athens

31 The theatre of Herodes Atticus at Athens

(see illustration 31). It was built next to the theatre of Dionysus. The elaborate arches built behind the stage, which are typical of Roman theatres, can still be seen.

As these theatres were built, the popularity of theatre-going increased. But what did the audiences see? Generally, there was less serious drama and more of the sensational exhibitions which were designed to appeal to Roman crowds. One writer, Seneca, composed several tragedies, but not for performance. Like many aristocratic Romans, he despised the theatre as it now was, and the other popular entertainments. Seneca therefore wrote his plays to be read aloud to select audiences, not for the stage. His tragedies were based on those by the Greek writers, and he used the legends they had used. Like Sophocles, he wrote a play called *Oedipus*, in which he told of the blinding of the king of Thebes. Seneca brought out the bloodthirsty and violent elements in the story with horrific and lurid descriptions. His plays were widely read and greatly admired, both in his lifetime and long afterwards. With those of Plautus and Terence, they influenced writers long after the Roman theatres had closed.

The building of stone theatres was accompanied by the growth of huge oval amphitheatres, like the Colosseum in Rome. In these, bloody gladiatorial combats took place. The crowds loved them, as they also loved the chariot-races at the long racecourses known as 'circuses'. The theatre therefore had to cater for those who loved blood and excitement.

32 The Colosseum in Rome

Some emperors were also devoted to these shows, especially Nero, who thought himself a great singer and actor. He did not take part in performances of the great plays of the past. Instead, there were dramatic recitations of vivid and gory scenes. What the people most liked was to see death, and so this is what they were given. Condemned criminals or slaves were actually killed on stage as part of the performances. The same principle applied to sex. Live sexual exhibitions on stage were an invention of the Romans. It all seems a long way from the original theatres. People no longer wanted imagination, convention, illusion. They wanted the theatre not to imitate life, but to *be* life. The masks were really taken off now.

THE PANTOMIME

One final highlight of the theatre under the emperors was the *pantomime*, which developed partly from the original *mime*. The central figure was a masked dancer, who performed scenes with no words, accompanied by a musician with pipes. Poor poets could make a great deal of money from writing lyrics for the chorus who sang in the background. The central actor, a handsome, athletic figure, wore a graceful silk costume, and his movements were artistic and flowing.

Although he acted out scenes from Greek mythology, his appeal was very different from that of the tragic actors. Like a modern pop-singer, he attracted vast numbers of fans (of both sexes), who practically worshipped him. One pantomime actor, Paris, had a love-affair with the emperor's wife, which caused her to be banished; he himself was executed. On his tombstone was an inscription he composed himself. He called himself 'the glory of the theatre'.

THE END OF ROMAN THEATRE

The theatre under the emperors was far from dead. The splendid theatre buildings were frequently full. Slaves known as 'comic actors' entertained guests at the banquets of the rich. But once Christianity spread and gained power in the Empire, theatre-going was heavily criticised as immoral. Finally, in the sixth century AD, the Christian emperor Justinian closed down the theatres – though he was married to a mime actress, Theodora, whose strip-tease act had been very popular.

THE PLAYS GO UNDERGROUND

After the fall of the Roman Empire came the period known as the 'Dark Ages'. The invasions of barbarians from the north and east practically put a stop to the study of literature and the other arts. But some Greek and Roman manuscripts survived, and monks spent their lives copying them out, often not understanding what they were writing. Probably the mime actors, barred from performing in theatres, acted in country districts and simple settings, keeping alive the traditions and characters of the old theatre.

THE RENAISSANCE

The Renaissance (literally, 'rebirth') was the period when an interest in creating works of art and literature reawakened in Europe, partly through the study of Greek and Roman writings. It really began towards the end of the fourteenth century AD, and by the fifteenth, Italian writers were producing Latin plays, influenced by the Roman playwrights. In Italy there were performances of the Roman comedies: the Pope watched Plautus' *The Menaechmi* at the Vatican in 1502. The movement spread to Germany, Holland and England, helped by the invention of printing. Oxford and Cambridge universities and famous English schools started to perform Roman plays. In 1527 St Paul's School in London produced *The Menaechmi*, and the following year Terence's *Woman from Andros* (*Andria*). Seneca's influence was also felt. His horrific, gruesome tragedies were copied in Italian plays of the sixteenth century.

SHAKESPEARE

In this same period, Seneca's plays were also being read and, at last, performed in England. Shakespeare was strongly influenced by them. In *Hamlet*, Polonius says: 'Seneca cannot be too heavy nor Plautus too light.' Playwrights thought the Roman writers were ideal models to follow. Shakespeare's tragedies (*King Lear*, for example) contain bloody scenes, stories of revenge and violence. Despite the fact that he was said to know 'small Latin and less Greek', Shakespeare certainly read plays by Plautus and Terence in Latin at school; they were part of the basic curriculum. *The Comedy of Errors* is based largely on Plautus' *The Menaechmi* and *Amphitryo*, and in many other comedies ideas were taken from New Comedy. There are exchanges of character, mistaken identity, long-lost children being reunited, and many other ingredients now familiar to us from the Romans. Some characters even have names from Roman plays: in *The Taming of the Shrew* there are servants called Tranio and Grumio. Shakespeare also uses the stock characters such as the boasting soldier. The most famous of these is Falstaff, in *Henry IV*.

OTHER INFLUENCES

The Romans also influenced other English writers of Shakespeare's day, for example Marlowe and Ben Jonson, and eighteenth-century writers like Sheridan. In France in the seventeenth century, Molière's comedies owed much to Roman comedy, and the tragedies of Corneille and Racine were modelled on those of the Greeks. In Italy, the *Commedia dell' Arte*, which had a number of famous characters like Harlequin and Columbine, had ideas which seem to go right back to the very earliest examples of the Italian theatre, the Atellan plays.

Even theatre buildings showed the influence of the ancient theatre. The Globe Theatre in London, used by Shakespeare, was a different shape and style, but Shakespeare, like Sophocles, wrote for an open-air theatre, with little scenery to assist him. Both relied on the actors' words and the audience's imagination, not on tremendous scenic effects like those sometimes found in modern theatres. In many places, theatres followed Greek and Roman designs. The Italian architect Palladio based the Teatro Olympico at Vicenza in Italy on the plans of the Roman architect Vitruvius.

THE TWENTIETH CENTURY

You might think that by now the effects of the ancient theatre would have worn off, since our own theatres and plays seem so different from those described in this book. But this is not true. Even today, many plays use the themes and ideas of the Greeks and Romans. A recent French writer, Giraudoux, called a play *Amphitryon 38*, because it was the thirty-eighth known play on the legend. Anouilh's *Antigone* was based closely on Sophocles' version, though with important changes of emphasis. The American playwright Eugene O'Neill wrote a play called *Mourning Becomes Electra*, after studying the plays of Aeschylus.

Even the style of theatre-building lives on. In London, the seating area at the Olivier Theatre (part of the new National Theatre) is very much like that of the theatre of Dionysus.

PERFORMANCES OF GREEK AND ROMAN PLAYS TODAY

With so many good translations of the Greek and Roman plays available, theatres often perform them today. Several excellent films have been made of the Greek tragedies: the Italian director Pasolini produced a gripping version of Sophocles' *Oedipus*. Television and radio have also brought the plays of Greece and Rome to today's audiences.

There are even productions which use the original language of the plays, mainly in schools and universities. In 1977, within the space of a couple of months, there were three fine performances of Greek plays in Cambridge and London. University students at Cambridge put on Sophocles' *Electra*, and King's College, London presented *The Clouds*. At Whitgift School, just outside London, the headmaster directed a performance of *Antigone*.

Perhaps the most famous performances in Greek are those at Bradfield College, Berkshire, in the open-air, Greek-style theatre. Westminster School in London still maintains a tradition of performances in Latin of the comedies of Plautus and Terence.

OTHER LINKS

These productions help to keep alive the spirit of the Greek and Roman theatre, but there are many other links, perhaps less obvious. Millions of people each year watch the comic operettas of Gilbert and Sullivan, but how many of them see the connection between them and the plays of Aristophanes or Plautus? The boasting soldiers who are stock characters in New Comedy, and also in Shakespeare, turn up yet again in several operas. *HMS Pinafore* and *The Gondoliers* both have plots based on mixing up babies at birth. When Gilbert makes fun of British law courts (*Trial by Jury*), politics (*Iolanthe*), or intellectuals (*Patience*), he is close to *The Acharnians*, *The Wasps* and *The Clouds*.

Coming right up to date, we have only to think of the many comedy programmes on television which owe their ideas to humour which, if not as old as the hills, is certainly as old as the ancient Greeks. As one example, has it occurred to you how many comedies make fun of people in uniform? Why is this, do you think? Can you see a link with Roman comedy? Or what about the popular impersonators? How do they compare with the plays of Aristophanes?

YOUR OWN GREEK OR ROMAN PLAY

Following this chapter, there are some suggestions for activities. Reading this book should have given you an idea of how it felt to watch or act in plays written a long time ago. But there is nothing better than taking part yourself. Why not put on a dramatic competition, or work out the performance of a Greek chorus, with costumes, music and movement? Why not even produce a whole play, or write one of your own based on those of the Greeks or Romans? There are more ideas in the Further Study section, but perhaps you can think up some of your own.

CONCLUSIONS

This chapter is called 'The End of an Era?'. In some ways, the theatre of the Greeks and Romans has gone for ever. Perhaps we shall never really understand what a Greek who attended the festival of the Great Dionysia felt, because for us going to the theatre is not a religious activity. It is difficult to imagine the thoughts of the Greek actor who played a dozen different parts in one day. And we have lost sight of the idea of theatre-going as something involving a very large proportion of society. Today only a minority of the population watch plays in theatres.

But not everything is remote or impossible to grasp. Audiences today still laugh at comedies and are moved by tragedies – in the theatre or the cinema, on radio or television. Perhaps there is more opportunity than ever before to take part in plays at school or in dramatic societies. Actors today may not wear masks, but the experience of acting is still much the same.

A long road leads from Athens and the theatre of Dionysus to the West End of London – but it will certainly go much farther, thanks to the continuing fascination of acting and the stage.

Appendix A Greek and Roman Names
and Terms

Some Greek and Roman names and terms are awkward to say in English, and the following is a rough guide on how to pronounce them. In each name one syllable is printed in italics. Stress this syllable and pronounce the others quickly and lightly, without exaggerating the sounds.

Playwrights:

Aeschylus	*Ee*-skil-us
Sophocles	*Soff*-ok-leez
Euripides	You-*rip*-id-eez
Aristophanes	Ari-*stoff*-an-eez

Characters:

Antigone

Antigone	An-*tig*-on-ee
Ismene	Iz-*mee*-nee
Eurydice	You-*rid*-iss-ee
Eteocles	*Et*-ee-ok-leez
Polynices	Polli-*ny*-seez

The Clouds

Strepsiades	Strep-*sy*-ad-eez
Pheidippides	Phy-*dip*-id-eez
Socrates	*Soc*-rat-eez

The Ghost-Story

Philolaches	Phil-o-*lak*-eez
Theopropides	Theo-*prop*-id-eez
Callidamates	Calli-*dam*-at-eez

Actors:

Heracleides	Herra-*cly*-deez
Tlepolemos	Tlee-*pol*-em-us
Dicaiarchos	Dik-eye-*ark*-us

Other names:

Dionysus	Dy-on-*eye*-sus
Semele	*Sem*-el-ee
Clytemnestra	Cly-tem-*nest*-ra
Orestes	O-*rest*-eez
Oedipus	*Ee*-dip-us
Aristotle	*Ar*-iss-tottle
Acharnians	Ak-*arn*-ee-anz
Trygaios	Trig-*eye*-us

	Lysistrata	Ly-*sis*-tratta
	Alcmena	Alc-*mee*-na
	Menaechmi	Men-*ike*-mee
	Pyrgopolynices	Pergo-polli-*ny*-seez
Technical terms:	Dionysia	Dion-*eye*-see-a
	Lenaia	Len-*eye*-a
	orchestra	or-*kees*-tra
	skene	*skee*-nee
	parodos	*parr*-od-us
	mechane	*mee*-can-ee
	ekkyklema	ek-kik-*lee*-ma
	choregos	kor-*ee*-gus
	archon	*ar*-kon

Appendix B Plays and Playwrights

This Appendix contains the titles of Greek and Roman plays which have survived to the present day, and the names of their authors. In brackets are the approximate dates of the authors, and of the first performances of the plays (when we know these). If a play is named after a central character, this Greek or Roman name is given as the title; otherwise, the titles have been given an English translation.

GREEK TRAGEDY

Aeschylus (526–456 BC). First victory in a dramatic competition, 484 BC
The Persians (472); *Seven against Thebes* (467); *The Suppliants* (463); *Agamemnon, The Libation-Bearers, The Kindly Ones* (the Oresteian trilogy) (458); *Prometheus Bound*.

Sophocles (496–406 BC). First victory, 468 BC
Ajax; *Antigone* (441); *Oedipus*; *Women of Trachis*; *Electra*; *Philoctetes* (409); *Oedipus at Colonus*.

Euripides (485–406 BC). First victory, 440 BC
Rhesus; *Alcestis* (438); *Medea* (431); *Hippolytus* (428); *Children of Heracles*; *Andromache*; *Hecuba*; *Suppliant Women*; *Trojan Women* (415); *Electra* (413); *Helen* (412); *The Mad Heracles*; *Iphigenia among the Taurians*; *Ion*; *Phoenician Women*; *Orestes* (408); *Iphigenia at Aulis*; *The Bacchantes*.

GREEK COMEDY

Aristophanes (450–386 BC). First victory, 425 BC
The Acharnians (425); *The Knights* (424); *The Clouds* (423); *The Wasps* (422); *Peace* (421); *The Birds* (414); *Lysistrata* (411); *Women at the Thesmophoria* (411); *The Frogs* (405); *Women in the Assembly* (392); *Wealth* (388).

Menander (342–290 BC). First victory, 317 BC
The Bad-Tempered Man (317); parts of *The Arbitrants* and *Woman from Samos*.

ROMAN COMEDY

Plautus (240–180 BC)
The Donkeys; *The Pot of Gold*; *Amphitryo*; *The Bacchis Sisters*; *The Prisoners*; *Casina*; *The Little Box*; *Curculio*; *Epidicus*; *The Menaechmi*; *The Merchant*; *The Swaggering Soldier*; *The Ghost-Story*; *The Persian*; *The Little Carthaginian*; *Pseudolus*; *The Rope*; *Stichus*; *Three Pieces of Silver*; *Truculentus*; *The Travelling Bag*.

Terence (184–160 BC)
Woman from Andros (166); *The Mother-in-Law* (165); *The Self-Torturer* (163); *The Eunuch* (161); *Phormio* (161); *The Brothers* (160).

ROMAN TRAGEDY

Seneca (4 BC–AD 65)
Hercules; *Trojan Women*; *Phoenician Women*; *Medea*; *Phaedra*; *Oedipus*; *Agamemnon*; *Thyestes*.

Appendix C　The Greek Alphabet

Even if you do not know the Greek language, the Greek alphabet is quite easy to learn, and may be very useful. You have seen several examples of it in this book. It is also used in mathematics, and of course in modern Greece. Notice that Greek has seven vowels, with a short *e* and a long *e*, and a short *o* and a long *o*.

Capital letter	Small letter	English equivalent
A	α	a (h*a*t)
B	β	b
Γ	γ	g (*g*et)
Δ	δ	d
E	ϵ	e (b*e*t)
Z	ζ	z
H	η	$\bar{\text{e}}$ (b*ee*)
Θ	ϑ	th
I	ι	i (h*i*t)
K	κ	k, c (*c*at)
Λ	λ	l
M	μ	m
N	ν	n
Ξ	ξ	x
O	o	o (h*o*t)
Π	π	p
P	ρ	r
Σ	σ (ς)	s
T	τ	t
Y	υ	u, y
Φ	ϕ	ph
X	χ	ch (lo*ch*)
Ψ	ψ	ps (li*ps*)
Ω	ω	$\bar{\text{o}}$ (g*o*)

Further Study

BOOKS TO READ

For teachers

The number of books is colossal. For festivals, performances and costume, see especially A. W. Pickard-Cambridge's enormously thorough work *The Dramatic Festivals at Athens*, revised by J. Gould and D. M. Lewis (Oxford University Press 1968). R. C. Flickinger's *The Greek Theater and its Drama* (Chicago University Press 1918) is still very useful, and so is *An Introduction to the Greek Theatre* by P. D. Arnott (Macmillan 1959) – which could well be read by older pupils.

Among the books on tragedy and comedy, there are two excellent short works in the *Ancient Culture and Society* series, published by

Chatto & Windus: *The Greek Tragic Theatre*, H. C. Baldry (1971), and *The Comic Theatre of Greece and Rome*, F. H. Sandbach (1977). These are designed especially for sixth-formers or university students. H. D. F. Kitto's *Form and Meaning in Drama* (Methuen 1956) is a deservedly popular treatment of several plays, including *Antigone*, and R. Lattimore's *Story Patterns in Greek Tragedy* (Athlone Press 1964) has an interesting discussion of the plots. On Greek comedy, *Aristophanes* by Gilbert Murray (Oxford University Press 1933), *The Stage of Aristophanes* by C. W. Dearden (Athlone Press 1976), and *Aristophanic Comedy* by K. J. Dover (Batsford 1972) are all very well worth reading. On Roman comedy, W. Beare's *The Roman Stage* (Methuen 1969) is comprehensive, while also very interesting are *Roman Laughter* by E. Segal (Harvard University Press 1968), and G. E. Duckworth's *The Nature of Roman Comedy* (Princeton University Press 1962).

Many of these books are well illustrated, but the best collections of the visual evidence are in *The History of the Greek and Roman Theater* by M. Bieber (Princeton University Press 1961), and *Illustrations of Greek Drama* by A. D. Trendall and T. B. L. Webster (Phaidon 1971).

Of the numerous editions of the plays, two worthy of particular mention are *The Clouds* by K. J. Dover (Oxford University Press 1968), and Sophocles' *Electra* by J. H. Kells (Cambridge University Press 1973). Translations abound. Those in the Loeb Classical Library cover the whole range, but are not the most readable. The series *The Complete Greek Tragedies* (edited by D. Grene and R. Lattimore) (Chicago University Press 1953–9) is generally excellent, and there is a good translation of all of Aristophanes' comedies by P. Dickinson, in two volumes (Oxford University Press 1970). More suitable perhaps for acting are the Penguin versions, and of these *The Theban Plays* of Sophocles, by E. F. Watling, and the versions of *Wasps*, *Thesmophoriazusae*, *Frogs* (D. Barrett), and *Acharnians*, *Clouds*, *Lysistrata* (A. H. Sommerstein), are good examples of the series' virtues. Penguin also include Aristotle's *Poetics*, the *locus classicus* for theories of tragedy, in *Classical Literary Criticism* (T. S. Dorsch 1965). Two useful sets of translations by Kenneth McLeish are Sophocles: *Electra*, *Antigone*, *Philoctetes*; and Aristophanes, *Clouds*, *Women in Power*, *Knights* (Cambridge University Press 1978). A helpful introductory anthology, with some plays translated into English and extracts from others, is *Greek Drama for Everyman* by F. L. Lucas (Dent 1954).

Finally, there are two excellent surveys of the available literature in the series *New Surveys in the Classics* (Oxford University Press): *Greek Tragedy* by T. B. L. Webster (1971), and *Menander*, *Plautus*, *Terence* by W. G. Arnott (1975).

For pupils
A simple introduction is given in *The Greek Theatre* (*Aspects of Greek Life* series, Longman 1972) by Kenneth McLeish. The same author has also written the fuller, more detailed *Roman Comedy* (*Inside the Ancient World* series, Macmillan 1976). His simplified translations of several plays are in two books in *The Heritage of Literature*, a series by Longman. In *Four Greek Plays*, there is a version of *Antigone* which is certainly the most suitable for acting by younger pupils; the other collection is *The Frogs and Other Plays*.

Many books about the history of the theatre have a chapter on Greek and Roman theatre, such as *Discovering the Theatre* by C. V. Burgess (University of London Press 1960) and *The True Book about the Theatre* by A. Read (Muller 1964). There are excellent illustrations of the theatre throughout history in *Theatres: An Illustrated History* by S. Tidworth (Pall Mall Press 1973), and *World Theatre*, an illustrated history by Bamber Gascoigne (Ebury Press 1968).

There are several good books on the practical side of the theatre, such as *Your Book of Acting* by K. Nuttall (Faber 1957). This has helpful sections on 'Do's and don't's in the theatre', 'Making your own play' and 'How to produce a play'. A more detailed book along the same lines, and by the same author, is *Play Production for Young People*. Books like these often take examples from Greek or Roman plays.

If you want to take up the idea of making Greek or Roman costumes and masks, you can consult *Make a Mask* and *Making Costumes for School Plays* by Joan Peters and Anna Sutcliffe (Batsford 1970). These have many good practical ideas.

Many historical novels have been written about the Greeks and Romans. One dealing with the life of a Greek actor is *The Mask of Apollo* by Mary Renault (Longman 1968). *The Crown of Violet* by Geoffrey Trease (Macmillan 1961) has an imaginative, though not always accurate, account of a festival.

TOPICS FOR DISCUSSION

1 What kind of people become 'stars', and how? Are stars always the best at their particular activity? What kind of followers do stars have? Why do people follow them? Select the ten biggest stars you can think of, and compare your list with others in your class or group. Are they similar or different? Do any of them include actors or actresses? Why is this?

2 What are the advantages and disadvantages of an outdoor theatre? If you could build a theatre anywhere you wanted, what would it be like and why?

3 Look at the questions about *Antigone* on page 42. Discuss these, and find out how far you agree with each other. Was Antigone

right to bury her brother against Creon's orders? Are people right to refuse to fight when their country is at war? Are these cases similar or not? In what other situations can a person's conscience clash with the law?

4 Do you think there is too much sex in comedies or other plays today? Why is sex talked about so often? What about jokes to do with religion? Are there any other kinds of humour which can cause offence? Do you think people should be offended by jokes?

5 How much freedom of speech is there in England, in the theatre and on television and radio? How does this compare with the theatre of Aristophanes? Should there be any restrictions on what is said or shown on stage? Why?

SUBJECTS TO WRITE ABOUT

1 Choose one character from a modern comedy. Describe him or her in detail, mentioning appearance, personality and any other aspects you can think of. How does the actor show his own personality in playing this part? Do you think he is really like the character he plays? Why? What skills does an actor need to create a character different from himself?

2 Compare (with illustrations) the costume of a clown with that of a Greek comic actor. How different are they? Which is funnier to look at, and which is the more complete disguise?

3 Using the Greek alphabet (Appendix C), decipher what you can of the *Athenian Victors' List* on page 11. Using Greek letters, write the numbers 24, 13 and 7. Write in Greek the names of Antigonē, Haimōn and Creōn.

4 How did the English words *orchestra*, *scene*, *theatre* and *hypocrite* get their present meanings? How much have these words changed in meaning from the time of the Greeks? Why have these changes taken place?

5 Imagine that you have been appointed *choregos* for *Antigone*. Write a plan of your activities in the period leading up to the performance, describing how you intend to help Sophocles to win.

6 What kinds of occasion is it difficult to get tickets for today? How do people try to make sure of a ticket for such occasions?

7 Think of some present-day comedians who are particularly good at winning audiences over. How do they do it?

8 Answer the questions on page 71 about modern comedy.

EXPLORATION

1 What different festivals are celebrated today in (*a*) England, (*b*)

Italy, (c) Greece and (d) Spain? Choose one festival from each country and find out how it is celebrated.

2 Find out the names of playwrights who have recently written plays. Where are these plays advertised? How long do they usually run for? What have been the most successful or longest running plays in recent years?

3 How many film or play versions of English legends can you discover? Think of Robin Hood, King Arthur. Any others?

4 Take one comedy programme on radio or television and think of as many different kinds of humour as you can find in it – puns, visual humour, etc. What kinds of humour do you find most funny? Which are your favourite comedies? Why?

5 Try to use encyclopedias to discover other plays which have used ideas or characters from the ancient Greek and Roman theatre.

6 Discover what you can about the design of theatre buildings today, and how the theatres are organised. (If possible, visit a modern theatre, such as the National Theatre in London, to find this out.) How are the theatres financed? How much does it cost to go to the theatre? Where do the actors come from? What kinds of play are produced, who goes to the theatre, and what are the most popular forms of production?

ACTIVITIES

1 Make a model of the theatre of Dionysus, based on the plan and photograph on pages 20 and 27.

2 Sophocles invented the practice of painting the front wall of the *skene*. Do an illustration of the kind of painting you think would have been suitable for *Antigone*.

3 Study the full play *Antigone* and, working in a group of three, work out possible ways of dividing the characters between the three of you.

4 Imagine you are Dicaiarchos, playing the four parts in *Antigone* listed on page 33. Work out the four different characters, their voices, walks and personalities. See if your friends can tell which you are supposed to be simply from your movements, or from your voice.

5 Using illustrations from vase-paintings, or any others from books about the theatre, design and (if possible) make costumes for *Antigone*.

6 Using a book about masks, make a tragic or comic mask to suit any of the characters from the plays you have read about. (A group could make masks for all the characters in *Antigone*.)

7 Wearing a mask, work out how to show the audience that you are crying, laughing, astonished, horrified, puzzled. Can you think of other feelings you might want to convey? How would you do it?

8 Study the messenger-speech telling of the death of Antigone and Haimon. How would you make this dramatically effective? Movements? Tone of voice? Pauses? Changes of speed?

9 Look carefully at the picture of a scene from a comedy, on page 57, and write down what you think is happening in it. Compare your answer with the explanation given below. Design a scene from *The Clouds* to go on the side of a vase, and turn this into a vase-painting.

10 Construct a small working model of a *mechane*, which can hoist a miniature figure into the air.

11 Read a legend of the ancient Greeks, and write your own play (either a tragedy or comedy) based on it. Follow the Greek rules for the number of actors, use of chorus, and so on.

12 Act out a scene (or, if possible, more – or even the whole play) from one of the comedies of Aristophanes. Work out how to make it funny – but not, of course, silly – to the audience. Try to update some of the humour.

13 In a group of fifteen, work out properly how to perform a tragic chorus. (Other members of the class could be involved with music, making costumes and masks, and training the chorus.) Use a recorder or flute to accompany the music. One of the class may be able to compose suitable music. Think out the dances and other movements, and practise good unison effects, and variations in mood and volume. If you use the chorus from *Antigone* on page 37, the tune below may give you an idea. (Notice that on a piano only white notes are needed; but if each note is treated as a 'sharp', the tune can be played entirely on the five black notes of the scale.)

The picture on page 57

This is supposed to show an old miser who is being robbed by two thieves. The figure on the right, looking on, may be a rather useless slave. The old man sleeps on the large box containing his treasures, to protect them. The thieves are trying to pull him off, but are tugging in opposite directions.